S0-EVD-039

TRANSNATIONAL CORPORATIONS IN A DEVELOPING COUNTRY

TRANSNATIONAL CORPORATIONS IN A DEVELOPING COUNTRY

The Indian Experience

JOHN MARTINUSSEN

SAGE Publications
New Delhi • Newbury Park • London

Copyright © John Martinussen, 1988.

All rights reserved. No part of this book may be reproduced or utilised in any form or by any means, electronic or mechanical, including photocopying, recording, or by any information storage and retrieval system, without permission in writing from the publisher.

First published in 1988 by

Sage Publications India Pvt Ltd
32, M-Block Market, Greater Kailash I
New Delhi 110 048

Sage Publications Inc
2111 West Hillcrest Drive
Newbury Park, California 91320

Sage Publications Ltd
28 Banner Street
London EC1Y 8QE

Published by Tejeshwar Singh for Sage Publications India Pvt Ltd and printed at Chaman Offset Printers.

Library of Congress Cataloging in Publication Data

ISBN 0 – 8039 – 9584 – 9 (USA)
81 – 7036 – 121 – 4 (India)

Contents

List of Figures and Tables	6
List of Abbreviations and Explanation of Symbols	8
Preface	9
Introduction	11
Chapter 1 The Host Country's Dilemma	16
Chapter 2 Indian Policies Affecting Transnational Corporations	36
Chapter 3 Administration and Implementation of Indian Policies	60
Chapter 4 Effects of the Regulations on the Balance of Payments	94
Chapter 5 Effects of the Regulations on Transfer of Resources	135
Chapter 6 Effects of the Regulations on Allocation of Resources	164
Chapter 7 Summary and Discussion of Findings	182
Appendices	207
Selected Bibliography	222

039921

List of Figures and Tables

Figures

1. A Simplified Model of Resource Circulation Within a TNC — 18
2. Hypothesised Model of the Interrelationship Between Foreign Direct Investments and Host Country Attractiveness — 26
3. An Outline of the Coverage of the IDR Act, the MRTP Act, and FERA — 49
4. Outline of the Administration of Section 29 of FERA — 61
5. Outline of the Industrial Approval System After 1973 — 66
6. Net Inflow of Foreign Direct Investment, 1970-83 — 138
7. Number of Foreign Collaborations Approved and Foreign Equity Investment Involved, 1969-85 — 141
8. Foreign Investment Involved in Collaboration Agreements, 1970-86 — 146

Tables

3.1 The Implementation of Section 29 of FERA — Selected Data — 68
3.2 The Implementation of Section 29 of FERA — The Position as on Dec 31, 1982 — 69
3.3 The Implementation of Section 29 of FERA — The Position as on Dec 31, 1981, Regarding Pharmaceutical Companies — 74
3.4 Illustrative List Showing TNC-Affiliated Companies Producing More than Double Their Licensed Capacities — Selected Products (1979) — 86
4.1 Profitability Ratios for Foreign and Indian Controlled Companies, 1971-72 and 1972-73 — 96
4.2 Dividends Paid Abroad as a Percentage of Total Dividends Paid by Medium and Large Companies, 1975-76 — 98
4.3 Dividends Paid Abroad as a Percentage of Total Dividends Paid by 313 Foreign Controlled Rupee Companies, 1975-76 to 1980-81 — 99
4.4 Dividends Paid Abroad by Medium and Large Companies — Industry-wise (1975-1981) — 102
4.5 Foreign Exchange Utilisation by 313 Foreign Controlled Rupee Companies, 1975-76, 1979-80 and 1980-81 — 108
4.6 Remittances Made Abroad by Private Sector Companies, 1969-70 to 1978-79 — 109

List of Tables and Figures

4.7	Remittances Made Abroad by Private Sector Companies, 1969-70 to 1978-79	110
4.8	The Structure of Expenditure in Foreign Currency by Medium and Large Companies, 1975-76 to 1982-83	113
4.9	The Private Corporate Sector's Utilisation of Foreign Currency and Total Sales, 1975-76 to 1980-81	115
4.10	Imported to Total Raw Materials, Components, Stores and Spares Consumed, 1975-76 to 1977-78	117
4.11	Imported to Total Raw Materials, Components, Stores and Spares Consumed by 313 Foreign Controlled Rupee Companies, 1975-76 to 1980-81	118
4.12	Earnings in Foreign Exchange to Net Sales for Indian and Foreign Controlled Companies, 1975-76 to 1977-78	120
4.13	Earnings and Expenditure in Foreign Exchange of 313 Foreign Controlled Rupee Companies, 1975-76, 1979-80 and 1980-81	124
4.14	Foreign Exchange Utilisation and Earnings by 190 Foreign Controlled Companies, 1980-81 and 1983-84	125
4.15	Earnings and Expenditure in Foreign Exchange of Indian and Foreign Controlled Companies	126
4.16	Earnings and Expenditure in Foreign Exchange of FCRCs According to the Country of Controlling Interest, 1975-76 to 1977-78 and 1979-80 to 1980-81	127
4.17	Earnings and Expenditure in Foreign Currency by the Corporate Sector, 1975-76 to 1982-83	128
5.1	Dilution of Foreign Equity Holdings by FERA Companies, 1976-80	136
5.2	Index of Industrial Production, 1974-81	140
5.3	Profitability Ratios for Foreign Controlled Companies, 1975-76 to 1980-81	140
5.4	Foreign Participation in Respect of Capital Issues Approved, 1976-80	143
5.5	Number of Foreign Collaborations Approved, Selected Countries, 1970-1982	151
5.6	Sectors of Concentration in India's Foreign Collaboration by Country	152
6.1	Foreign Investment by Industry, 1948, 1961, 1974 and 1980	167
6.2	Approved Foreign Collaborations — Industry-wise, Four-year Periods, 1970-85	168
App.V	A. The Structure of Expenditure in Foreign Currency. Chemicals. 1975-76 to 1980-81	219
App.V	B. The Structure of Expenditure in Foreign Currency. Engineering. 1975-76 to 1980-81	220
App.V	C. The Structure of Expenditure in Foreign Currency for Group III — Industries, 1975-76 to 1980-81	221

List of Abbreviations and Explanation of Symbols

CTC	Center for Transnational Corporations
ECOSOC	Economic and Social Council
EPW	Economic and Political Weekly
ESCAP	Economic and Social Council for Asia and the Pacific
FCRC	Foreign Controlled Rupee Companies
FERA	Foreign Exchange Regulation Act
FIB	Foreign Investment Board
IDR Act	Industrial (Development and Regulation) Act
IMF	International Monetary Fund
LDC	Less Developed Countries
MRTP Act	Monopolies and Restrictive Trade Practices Act
OECD	Organisation for Economic Cooperation and Development
ONGC	Oil and Natural Gas Commission
OPPI	Organisation of Pharmaceutical Producers of India
PAB	Project Approval Board
RBI	Reserve Bank of India
SIA	Secretariat for Industrial Approval
TNC	Transnational Corporation
UN	United Nations
UNCTC	United Nations Centre for Transnational Corporations
UNCTAD	United Nations Conference on Trade and Development
UNIDO	United Nations Industrial Development Organisation

...	Data not available
–	Magnitude nil or less than half of the unit employed
	Category not applicable
1 lakh	100,000
1 million	1,000,000
1 crore	10,000,000
1 billion	1,000,000,000

Preface

During the period from 1969 to 1974, the Indian government evolved a new regulatory framework pertaining to activities of foreign controlled companies in the country. This book reviews and assesses the new policies pursued after 1974 with particular emphasis on the effects on the activities of transnational corporations. The approach adopted is presented in Chapter 2 and 3 of the book. An executive summary of the major findings, with references to supporting evidence, is included in Chapter 7.

The reviews and assessments are based primarily on studies carried out in India in 1977, 1979, 1983 and 1988. In conducting these studies I benefitted immensely from cooperation extended by Indian scholars and research institutions. I am indebted to so many that it would be impossible to name them all here. Some of them, however, qualify for special attention. This applies to Professor Amiya Bagchi, Subhendu Dasgupta, Uttam Bhattacharya and Sudip Chaudhuri, all of the Centre for Studies in the Social Sciences, Calcutta; Professor S.K. Goyal, Nagesh Kumar, Kamal Chenoy and other present and former members of the Corporate Studies Group, Indian Institute of Public Administration, New Delhi; Dr. K.K. Subramanian and Mohanan Pillai, Sardar Patel Institute of Economic and Social Research, Ahmedabad.

I also want to express my deep gratitude to the more than 100 business representatives and government officials, who readily answered my questions during comprehensive and often protracted interviews. Several of those interviewed in 1977 or 1979 even granted me another interview in 1983, thus facilitating the identification of changes in policies pursued by the government as well as changes in the business environment in which the policies were implemented. The Danish Embassy in New Delhi rendered very helpful assistance by arranging meetings with top government officials.

The basic outline of the assessments and analyses presented here were published in a report for restricted circulation in 1986. The present book, however, is a completely revised version of this report. Major arguments have been developed further and new data have been included wherever appropriate.

In this connection I want to express my appreciation of the Indian Investment Centre, New Delhi, for furnishing all the updated information requested. A special acknowledgment must be addressed to the Corporate Studies Group at the Indian Institute of Public Administration for giving me free access to their extensive data files, newspaper clippings and collection of company annual reports.

The research in India has been financed primarily by the Danish Research Council for Development Research. Research in Denmark has been financed by the University of Aarhus and Roskilde University Centre. My participation in a particularly inspiring conference on the impact of transnational corporations on India's position in the international division of labour, in January 1988, was funded by the Indo-Dutch Programme on Alternatives in Development.

March 1988
John Martinussen

Introduction

Less developed countries (LDCs) have put forward demands for a new international economic order which, among other things, would give them a significantly greater share of the World's industry - generally around 25 per cent by the year 2000 - as well as a correspondingly greater proportion of World trade in industrial goods.

A cursory glance at some of the current estimates of global industrial development and trade between less developed and developed countries could give the immediate impression that the demands mentioned are being gradually complied with. Thus, available information indicates that there has been, during the last 10 to 15 years, a considerable growth, absolutely and relatively, in the industrial production of LDCs. The data also indicate an increase in their exports of industrial products. These changes have been duly emphasised by representatives of developed countries' governments and large international organisations, notably the World Bank.

The possibility remains, however, that this whole formulation of the issue in terms of traditional economics might obscure more than it reveals. This, at least, is the opinion of some of the most prominent representatives of the LDCs. It is also the opinion of a number of social scientists, who emphasise that the perceived changes are, to a great extent, the results of an augmentation of foreign-controlled industry in LDCs. Furthermore, it is this foreign-controlled industry which, above all, accounts for the growth in industrial exports from LDCs. Dissimilarities obviously exist between countries, but the foreign-controlled part of industry is probably nowhere less than 10 per cent, the typical percentage lying above 30.[1]

In addition, foreign control is often more prevalent in the most dynamic and expanding sectors and with regard to products of great strategic importance for accumulation and reproduction. It generally occurs, for instance, that foreign companies control between 60 and 80 per cent of machine industry. Furthermore, there is much to indicate, as regards industrial exports, that nearly half of these take place in the form of intra-firm trade controlled by transnational corporations' (TNCs') head offices in the developed countries.

Bearing this in mind, the above-mentioned changes cannot forthwith be interpreted as advances towards a realisation of the demands for a new international economic order. Only closer analyses can substantiate whether the changes actually correspond to the intentions behind the demands. Such careful analyses should aim at demolishing conventional ideas of nation-states as the only important actors and units of analysis in the global economic and political systems. They should, instead, perceive of both global and national economic and political processes as being shaped and managed jointly by nation-states and TNCs.

Conceptions like these have formed, in the last decade, the basis of a growing number of studies. Quite often, their focus has been on the role of TNCs.[2] These studies have left the general impression that the activities of

TNCs have frequently engendered a series of undesired effects in LDCs, as seen from their point of view. There has been no agreement as to the specific effects of the corporations, nor as to whether the benefits have offset the drawbacks. In any case, the studies have pointed out the desirability of regulating the TNCs' activities in order to extract the greatest possible benefits for the further economic and social development of LDC host countries.

From these premises has issued a steadily intensifying debate about international codes of conduct for TNC activities and business practices. Apart from the United Nations, this debate has taken place especially within the OECD and other international bodies, as well as among social scientists. The debate has mainly turned on the need for rules to govern the activities of TNCs, with the further aim of protecting the corporations themselves against 'unsound' and 'unfair' competition, and of reducing the often demonstrated detrimental effects in both developed and less developed countries.

The merits of looking closer at these problems cannot be questioned. The notion lingers, nevertheless, that this debate - as seen from LDC host countries' point of view - has concerned itself more with principles and precepts than with the problems of enforcing these through concrete measures. In this context it should be borne in mind that it is ultimately the responsibility of each individual country's government to ensure that the TNCs comply with the adopted rules and regulations

This extremely important aspect of the regulation issue has been insufficiently researched. Documentation does indeed exist as regards the variety of laws and regulations different LDCs have enacted or tried to enforce with respect to TNC activities.[3] However, there is a dearth of thorough studies concerning the actual implementation or the wider effects of these laws and regulations. Consequently, little is known about the interrelationships between objectives, means and effects in this field. In other words, neither social scientists nor decision-makers in LDCs know much about which measures would be most appropriate in order to bring about certain desired effects.

The present book aims at penetrating deeper into this core of the regulation question. Empirically, the study concerns India. The major results, however, are presumed to have relevance and at least some validity for other LDCs and their endeavours at regulating and controlling TNC activities. In this way it is hoped that the study may contribute to the general understanding of the processes and problems involved in LDC governments' regulations of TNC operations.

Notes and References

1. The term 'LDCs' does not here include the socialist-oriented or non-capitalist countries of the Third World.
2. The United Nations Economic and Social Council (ECOSOC) should in particular be credited for launching, in the early 1970s, an extensive documentary research into the global economic importance and role of TNCs. Three publications warrant special attention: UN, Department of Economic and Social Affairs, *Multinational Corporations in World Development*, New York, 1973; UN, ECOSOC, *Transnational Corporations in World Development: A Re-examination*, New York, 1978; and UN Centre on Transnational Corporations, *Transnational Corporations in World Development, Third Survey*, New York, 1983.

3. Again ECOSOC and the UN Centre on Transnational Corporations have undertaken extensive compilation and analyses of available data; see especially UN Centre on Transnational Corporations, *National Legislation and Regulations Relating to Transnational Corporations*, New York, 1983. A previous survey was published in 1978.

• CHAPTER 1 •

The Host Country's Dilemma

LDCs are caught in a dilemma in their relations with TNCs. *On the one hand,* the TNCs can provide enormous financial resources for investment in LDCs. Not only do these corporations generate substantial financial resources internally, they also have privileged access to the international capital markets and financial institutions. Secondly, they can offer sophisticated technology and management skills not readily available from other sources. Thirdly, they command access to superior distribution and marketing systems suitable for increasing exports. Fourthly, TNC operations in LDCs can create employment. In other words, TNCs may indeed offer sizable net benefits to less developed countries.

On the other hand, it is commonly acknowledged that TNC activities may also imply great disadvantages and costs.[1] The actual inflow of capital may not be very large, not even in the initial stages of a direct investment project. It depends on the extent to which local capital markets are tapped in order to finance the project concerned. As regards the transfer of technology and management skills, these often involve excessively high costs, because TNCs take advantage of their monopolistic positions. Besides, the technology being transferred may not be appropriate to the factor endowment of the host countries. Frequently, the TNCs employ highly capital-intensive technology even in LDCs where capital is scarce and labour relatively abundant and cheap. As a consequence, the employment effects remain meagre.

Generally speaking, the TNCs do not necessarily provide capital, technology, employment opportunities or access to distribution and marketing facilities to any great extent. They may even, through their operations, bring about distortions in the host countries' economies and reduce the effectiveness of national development programmes and other economic policies.

Whether costs and disadvantages associated with TNC operations prevail over the benefits cannot be ascertained *a priori*. Costs and benefits vary greatly from host country to host country; from one branch of industry to another; even from one corporation to another. Furthermore, costs and benefits vary according to the forms of activity. Individual host countries may also experience significant changes over time.

Consequently, it is necessary to assess the contribution of TNCs on a case by case basis.[2] Host governments must evaluate each case in an effort to distinguish the positive and negative effects, both actual and prospective.[3]

Some of the reasons for this 'open' approach may be inferred from a simplified model of the resource circulation within a TNC with a branch or subsidiary in a less developed country. Using this model as a point of reference, we may also be able to bring about a systematic, albeit not very sophisticated, first account of some of the major problems involved in the regulation of TNC activities.

A Simplified Model of Resource Circulation Within a TNC

In the *first stage* of the resource circulation

process, outlined here in Figure 1, a certain amount of money capital is transferred from a parent company in a highly developed country to an LDC. The purpose may be to take over the control of an existing firm or to establish a branch or subsidiary in the country concerned.

Figure 1

A Simplified Model of Resource Circulation Within a TNC

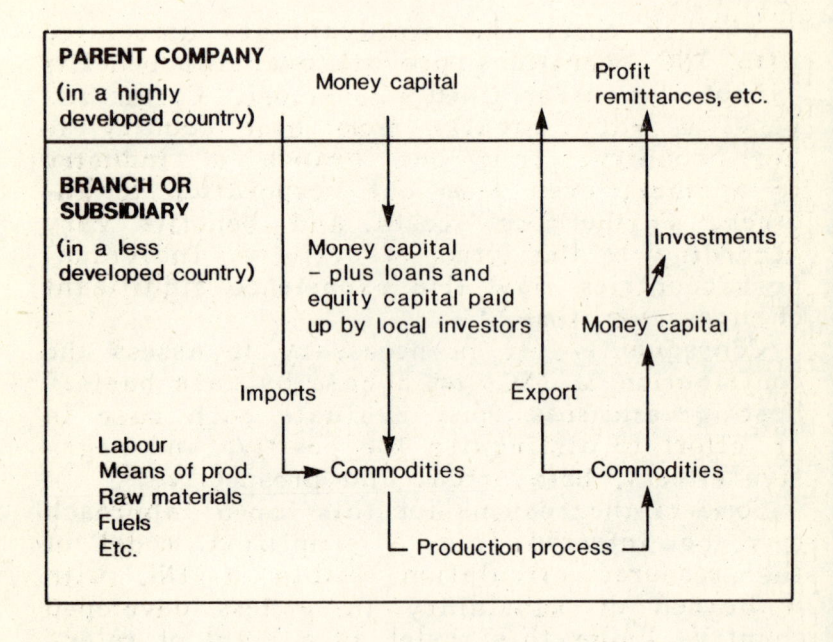

PARENT COMPANY (in a highly developed country)	Money capital ↓	Profit remittances, etc. ↑
BRANCH OR SUBSIDIARY (in a less developed country)	Money capital – plus loans and equity capital paid up by local investors ↓	Investments ↗ Money capital ↑
Labour, Means of prod., Raw materials, Fuels, Etc.	Imports → Commodities ↓	Export ← Commodities ↑
	└── Production process ──┘	

It is assumed in the model that the TNCs engage directly in production. Cases where TNCs invest only in the sphere of circulation, i.e., trade and finance, or where they participate in production only through technical collaboration agreements, are included in the sense that they correspond to selected aspects of the resource circulation process as described.

The money capital transferred in the first stage may constitute only a minor share of the total capital invested, the rest being provided by local financial institutions or paid up by local investors. As a result, detrimental effects may occur in the form of preempting host-country savings, thus preventing local firms from obtaining funds for some of their projects. In this sense, TNC borrowing in host countries may displace local initiative and activity.

The *second stage* of the circulation process involves the buying of the inputs necessary for the production process, i.e., labour, means of production, raw materials, fuels, intermediate goods, technology not embodied in machinery, etc. These inputs may to some extent be imported from the parent company, in which case the TNC in question is in a position to transfer resources from the subsidiary to the parent company. This may be done through over-pricing the imported inputs, more specifically, by charging higher prices than those prevailing in the world market for the same commodities, services, labour or know-how.

In addition to this kind of resource transfer, a TNC may also benefit substantially from what is sometimes termed 'over-exploitation' of local labour. The expression refers to situations where local labour is obtained at prices below the costs of reproducing the labour in a family context. Thus, part of the physical reproduction of the workers' families is taken care of by other forms of economic activity - typically through the families cultivation of small plots of land.

After the production process, which constitutes the *third stage*, the resource circulation process enters the *fourth stage* where the products are sold in the domestic or foreign markets. To the extent that the subsidiary sells commodities or services to the parent company, this provides the corporation with yet another possibility of transferring resources as the commodities and services may be sold at prices significantly below those prevailing in the world market. Even if this 'under-pricing' in intra-firm trade does not take place, the corporation is still left with opportunities for transferring resources in the form of profit remittances or disinvestments.

Whether any transfer of resources from the branch or subsidiary to the parent company actually takes place cannot be ascertained *a priori*. It depends on several factors, the most influential of which relate to the conditions of capital accumulation and long-term profit maximisation in a national as well as a global perspective. The same factors partly determine the extent to which a TNC will apply its global distribution and marketing systems to increase exports from the LDCs where it is operating.

The open approach indicated here is based upon a growing number of empirical studies. These have shown that the socio-economic impact of TNC activities are too complex and too dependent on several determinants to be generalised in simple terms. Neither the dependency theory nor the modernisation theory - including the so-called 'mainstream' economic theory - has produced generally valid conclusions in this field.

This does not prevent us, however, from advancing general propositions regarding basic determinants governing TNC behaviour. In the present context, the important feature to note is that profitability considerations and other determining interests of a TNC are located in the parent company – not in the branch or subsidiary. Furthermore, the parent company wields effective control over affiliates, if it wants to. Control may be exercised in a number of ways, including direct managerial control and financial control.[5]

Under these circumstances, the process of resource circulation and capital accumulation within a TNC is basically externally determined, looked at from the point of view of the host country. This remains so, even if we accept that the overall objective for a TNC is not simply a short-term maximisation of profits in the parent company, but rather a combination of long-range maximisation – or perhaps merely optimisation – and continuous expansion of operations.[6] Under certain conditions, these objectives may be best taken care of by maximising the profits of the branch or subsidiary and by enlarging its operations. But – and this is the major point here – the whole question of how and where resources are allocated and used within a TNC is decided on the basis of the parent company's interests, not on the basis of those of the branch or subsidiary. The methods and the specific ranking of interests and priorities vary according to the organisation of the TNC and its strategies with regard to control, decision-making and expansion, but the basic proposition still remains valid.[7]

In this perspective it becomes quite obvious that, looked at from the point of view of indigenous social forces in less developed host countries, it is necessary to establish some sort of control over the operations of TNCs.

Problems of Host Government Regulations

There is no agreement with respect to what kind of regulations are the most appropriate for LDC host governments to enforce. Representatives of different social forces and interests advocate different kinds of regulations. They all seem to accept, however, that the host country must aim for a surplus of benefits over costs from the operations of TNCs. In the case of India, it also seems that the most important interest groups accept the basic purpose to be one of sustaining and accelerating the internally-oriented industrial development, while concomitantly reducing the external dependence.[8] This need not imply exclusion of TNCs from operating in India. On the contrary, it is widely acknowledged that the corporations may indeed contribute substantially to industrial development, provided their activities are shaped accordingly by means of effective government controls.

In agreement with this conception we will use the terms 'regulation' and 'control' in a wider sense to denote government interventions which produce, or at least intend to produce, a higher degree of internally-oriented industrial development. In a narrow sense the terms will refer to interventions which aim at minimising detrimental effects and costs, and maximising the beneficial effects of TNC operations.[9]

In this context, the problems facing the decision-makers in India, as in other LDCs, are essentially how to manipulate societal conditions in such a way that the TNCs are either forced to, or acquire an interest in, providing larger financial resources, more adequate technology at lower costs, access to global distribution and marketing systems, and other resources in the broadest sense of the term. In addition, it is a question of how to influence the flows of capital, technology, and other resources in such a way that the impact on the internally-oriented industrial development is optimised.[10]

The tasks, in other words, imply the designing of a comprehensive set of economic and regulatory policies towards TNCs which will improve their contributions to growth within priority sectors, employment, balance of payments, tax revenues, transfer of technology, training, and economic independence in general.

It is worthy of note that with this conceptualisation the problems of regulation cannot be reduced to problems of limiting TNC activities as much as possible. A simplification of this kind would apply only to activities with no positive net effects in the sense outlined above. As a principle, activities of this kind should be discontinued. This may be difficult, however, due to the fact that the TNCs concerned are often engaged in other operations with a beneficial impact. Consequently, they could retaliate by closing down such operations to the detriment of the host country's industrial development.[11]

This illustrates a more general problem: policies towards TNCs often imply conflicting objectives. It may be helpful, therefore, to draw a distinction between at least four basically different policy objectives.

The *first* is to attract foreign involvement. A minimum of investment opportunities and business prospects are prerequisites for attracting TNC investments or other desirable forms of involvement in a host country's economic development. In order to attract *different* types of involvement, different sets of policies may be required.[12]

Emphasis on factors and policies of attraction may be related to commonly stated advantages that foreign investment has over borrowing from foreign commercial banks. One such advantage is that equity financing requires payments to be made only when the investment earns a profit, whereas debt requires payments irrespective of the financial results. Another advantage is that payments under foreign direct investment can - at least in principle - be regulated by host country authorities while debt payments are almost completely outside their control.[13]

These and other advantages must, however, be judged against certain disadvantages associated with foreign direct investment. The subject is discussed below.

The *second* policy objective is to ensure an appropriate selection of TNC involvement in keeping with development priorities.

The *third* objective is to obtain a stronger bargaining position *vis-à-vis* the TNCs. This may refer to new foreign investors or established affiliates wishing to expand their activities. In both cases, the aim is to extract more net benefits from the corporations' activities.

The *fourth* policy objective is to maximise net benefits from on-going TNC activities by tightening controls and operating conditions. TNCs have always strongly objected against such posterior alterations of regulatory policies, but because their bargaining positions have often been weakened once they have invested and established affiliates, this kind of policy changes has a certain appeal for host country governments.

Bearing these different policy objectives in mind, we may now return to the dilemma mentioned above. How should a government act in relation to TNCs engaged in operations which, for some reason or another, the government wants to preserve, albeit in a modified form and adapted to a greater extent to the country's development goals?

There are no ready answers to these and similar complicated questions. We may, however, acquire a little more insight into the problems involved by focusing our attention on direct investments for a moment. As is well known, this is only one among several forms of penetration applied by TNCs.[14] Nevertheless, it is contended here that the problems of regulating investment flows can serve as an illustration of the more complex problems of controlling other forms of TNC penetration. Besides, it is with respect to investment control that India, and almost all other LDCs, have implemented the most comprehensive and elaborate policy measures.

The problems of investment regulation within the framework outlined in the preceding paragraphs may be presented tentatively as in Figure 2. The reasoning behind the Figure can be summed up in this way:

When the financial managers of a TNC consider investing in a particular LDC, they have to take into account that their primary responsibilities are to allocate limited financial resources among competing investment projects, and to choose the least costly methods of financing new and ongoing operations.[15] In a wider perspective, this implies that a TNC will make the investment only on the condition that the country concerned offers a certain minimum of advantages and politically determined incentives. In the financial managers' comparatively narrow perspective, this minimum is translated into the minimum acceptable rate of return on investment, based on considerations of capital costs and the specific risks inherent in the proposed investment. But not only that. The financial managers

Figure 2
Hypothesised Model of the Interrelationship Between Foreign Direct Investments and Host Country Attractiveness

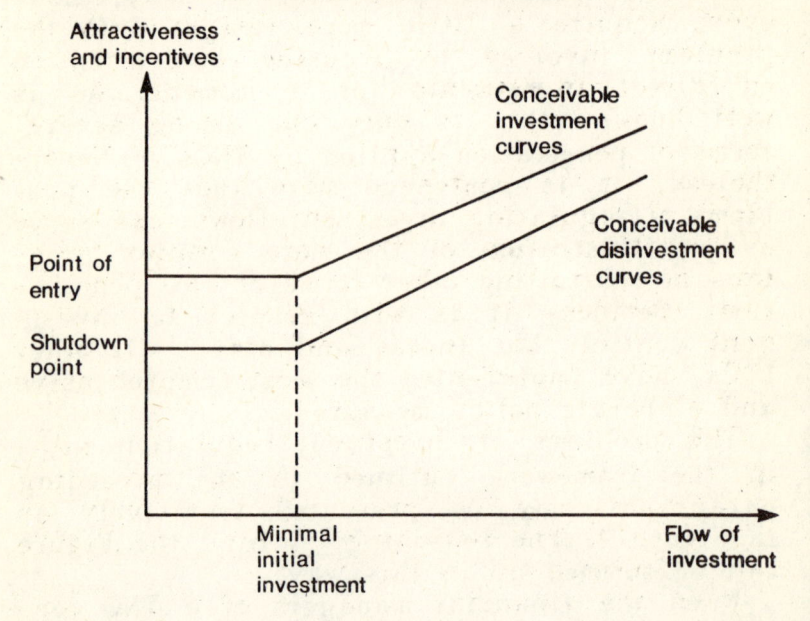

also have to consider the proposed investment against alternative uses of the investment funds, i.e., the opportunity costs.

In other words, the minimum required will depend on conditions prevailing in the corporation's home country as well as in alternative host countries. It will also depend on the corporation's investment strategy, risk analysis and project evaluation strategy - just to mention some of the most critical variables.[16]

The said minimum is shown in Figure 2 as 'the point of entry'. For reasons of simplification, it is assumed that the attractiveness of the country in question and the incentives provided by its government can be combined and indexed on one dimension. It is further assumed that a certain minimum initial investment is necessary for starting the operations.

The Figure suggests that provided the host country can offer attractiveness and incentives beyond or above the point of entry, this will bring about increased investments. The exact interrelationship cannot be specified as it varies greatly according to the kind of activity and the investment strategy, as presumably also from one host country to another. In the present context, however, the exact interrelationship is not essential. The major point is the basic contention that foreign investment will increase with increasing attractiveness.

Applying this reasoning in a situation where the government of an LDC is in favour of promoting TNC investments in certain high-priority sectors, it becomes a matter of how to manipulate the relevant attractions - to the extent that these can be manipulated by the government - and incentives in such a manner that the composite index rises above the point of entry. How far beyond this point the government should attempt to go would depend on a calculation of costs and benefits resulting from the increased TNC engagement. It is a question of approaching an optimal situation, looked at from the point of view of the host country, i.e., a situation in which the TNC activities concerned contribute as much as possible to the internally-oriented industrial development, while concomitantly inflicting as few as possible costs and disadvantages on the country.

If a situation of the said kind has been brought about, be it optimal or only sub-optimal, and if the TNCs have undertaken the relevant investments, it is further implied in Figure 2 that the host country authorities can then implement regulations and restrictions to a certain degree - without consequences for the size of the investment. This contention is indicated by the separate curves for investments and disinvestments and by the location of the shutdown point below the point of entry. The contention is based on the conventional understanding that when an investment has been undertaken, it requires a significant deterioration in conditions before disinvestment is initiated - at least in the short run.

If these propositions are valid, it implies that the host government can, to some degree, enforce regulations and restrictions in order to reduce the costs and disadvantages without affecting the size of foreign investments, provided these investments have been undertaken. It is very difficult, though, to determine the optimal situation as well as the exact margin for manoeuvring. Just to determine the effects of TNC operations in various respects, let alone balancing and weighing these effects, would require extensive research. Add to this the problems of predicting how the TNCs would actually respond to changes in attractiveness and incentives - a project that would require not only knowledge of the corporations' *real* priorities and investment policies, but also involve analyses of conditions in other countries where the TNCs concerned could alternatively place their investments.[17]

Disregarding these difficulties for the present, we may carry the reasoning behind the model in Figure 2 a little further by pointing out four overall strategies which can be applied by a host-country government in order to approach an optimal situation in the sense outlined above. Stated briefly, the strategies can be described in this way:

(a) First of all, the host-country government can intervene in a manner that renders superfluous specific TNC activities. In the terms of our simplified model, these activities then no longer have positive net effects and, consequently, should be discontinued. More specifically, the government may pursue this overall strategy either by supporting expansion of private, indigenous business at the expense of TNCs, or by establishing public sector undertakings to replace TNC operations. Of course, the same aim may be pursued by importing the products hitherto manufactured by TNC affiliates - or by substituting the items.

(b) Secondly, the government can contribute to the attractiveness of the host country by improving the basic economic and social conditions, e.g., by developing infrastructure or by 'disciplining' the labour force. Similarly, the attractiveness may be augmented by changing the politically determined incentives in favour of TNCs, e.g., by means of extended tax exemptions and other selective regulations.

(c) Thirdly, the government can enact specific regulations and restrictions with a view to minimise costs and disadvantages from TNC activities, at the same time maximising the gains and benefits.[18] In terms of our model, these forms of intervention may take advantage of the separation of - and the distance between - the investment and disinvestment curves.

(d) Finally, the government of a host country can help to render superfluous its own regulations and restrictions by supporting indigenous business in general and the most competitive part thereof in particular.

As pointed out above, direct investment is only one among several forms of engagement and penetration applied by TNCs in less developed countries.

We shall not discuss these other forms at

great length in the present context. Basically, it is assumed here that the problems of regulation in connection with these other TNC activities may be understood within conceptual frameworks similar to the one outlined. It is worth noting, though, that other forms of engagement are probably not characterised by the same inertia as direct investments. Consequently, the corresponding curves of engagement and disengagement may not be separated as far - if at all - as in the case of investment and disinvestment curves. Besides, the former curves presumably have significantly steeper slopes upwards and downwards than the latter, indicating that TNCs will generally respond to even marginal changes in conditions when it comes to non-financial forms of engagement and collaboration. This leaves the host government with correspondingly less scope for manoeuvring with respect to such other forms of TNC involvement. On the other hand, the potential advantages offered by the so-called new forms of investment to LDCs may be greater than those associated with direct foreign investment. Thus, it is quite conceivable that the new forms of investment show a greater responsiveness to host-government industrial policy measures, even when these measures do not include specific regulations relating to TNC activities.[19]

This hypothesis, if accepted, points to the need for analysing the determinants of the form of foreign engagement, the further aim being to influence the determinants in favour of non-equity forms of foreign involvement.

The feasibility and effectiveness of government interventions to that effect depend very much on the reasons why TNCs concerned have chosen direct investment in the first place as their mode of foreign involvement. Is it important for them to retain 'internalised' modes of involvement through direct ownership? Or would it be just as advantageous to change the mode of involvement and 'externalise'?[20]

These questions are of central importance when evaluating the effectiveness of Indian regulations after 1974.

From the same perspective, it is also worth noting that there has been, over the last 20 years, an overall tendency towards applying the so-called new modes of foreign involvement in LDCs. Larger and well-established TNCs have shown increased willingness to change their earlier involvement to forms other than foreign direct investment. Smaller and newer TNCs have at the same time shown remarkable willingness to become involved in LDCs in manners not associated with direct ownership and control.[21]

To the extent Indian regulations have aimed at reducing foreign direct control, the said tendency should be borne in mind when judging the effectiveness of the policies pursued. A distinction must be drawn between developments affected by Indian authorities and those overwhelmingly unaffected by host-country policies. Furthermore, the variations from one industry to another must be taken into account.[22]

Notes and References

1. Sanjaya Lall and Paul Streeten have provided a concise summary of what they term benefits and costs associated with TNC activities; see their *Foreign Investment, Transnationals and Developing Countries*, London, Macmillan, 1977, pp 53-77.
2. This approach has been recommended by the UN Centre on Transnational Corporations in their Third Survey. It has also been emphasized by a number of scholars; cf., e.g., Stefan H.Robock & Kenneth Simmonds, *International Business and Multinational Enterprises*, Homewood, Ill., Richard D.Irwin, 1983 (3rd. ed.), p 231.

3. This does not, however, preclude generalisations on the basis of existing empirical studies. My point is that substantially more research is required before we can draw generally valid conclusions. Even then the conclusions must vary according to the conditions under which the TNCs operate.

4. The model is based partly on the reasoning in Karl Marx's *Capital*, particularly Volume I, Chs. 21-23; partly on the literature concerning the organisation of TNCs, e.g., Robin Murray (ed.), *Multinationals Beyond the Market. Intra-firm Trade and Control of Transfer Pricing*, Brighton, The Harwester Press, 1981; and Michael Z.Brooke & H.Lee Remmers, *The Strategy of Multinational Enterprises. Organization and Finance*, London, Pitman, 1978.

5. Various aspects of control - and the implications for endeavours to attain legal control over TNC activities - are discussed in Cynthia Day Wallace, *Legal Control of the Multinational Enterprise*, The Hague, Martinus Nijhoff, 1983.

6. TNCs in general, and Japanese corporations in particular, often have sales growth and increasing market shares as their prime targets, especially in the early stages of a product life cycle. Profits are then expected to come from later market share leadership when the demand has grown and stabilised. Cf. Robock & Simmonds, *op.cit.*, p 447 ff.

7. On the different organisational set-ups and the multitude of strategies applied by the corporations, see, e.g., *ibid.*, Chs. 1-4, 6; Yoshi Tsurumi, *Multinational Management. Business Strategy and Government Policy*, Cambridge, Mass.,Ballinger,1984, Chs. 9-10; and Raymond Vernon, 'The Product Cycle Hypothesis in a New International Environment', *Oxford Bulletin of Economics and Statistics*, Vol. 41, No. 4 (1979), p 261 ff.

8. This general conclusion is based partly on written evidence, partly on discussions with representatives of various interest groups in India; see Appendix IV for further information. Views expressed by these representatives concerning the forms of control best suited to shape TNC activities are referred to later in this report.

9. This definition is basically in agreement with the one suggested by Cynthia Day Wallace in Wallace, *op.cit.*, p 23.

10. When we refer to industrial development here it is not to rule out the possibility that TNC activities relate primarily to agriculture or development in other sectors. The specific reference is based merely on the fact that TNC activities in India have been concentrated in mining, manufacturing, and related activities, all included here under the heading 'industrial'. Were we to take into account the impact of TNC operations on agricultural development, this could probably be done without altering the basic argument presented in the text above.

11. These remarks point to one of the major problems confronting decision-makers responsible for regulation of TNC activities, *viz.*, the fact that their primary concern is the specific activity and its impact, whereas the opposing TNC decision-makers are concerned with numerous activities under their command.

12. Cf. Friedrich von Kirchbach, *Economic Policies Towards Transnational Corporations. The Experience of the ASEAN Countries*, Baden-Baden, Nomos Verlagsgesellschaft, 1983, p A42.

13. These and other advantages are stressed by Pradumna B. Rana in 'Foreign Direct Investment and Economic Growth in the Asian and Pacific Region', *Asian Development Review*, Vol. 5, No. 1 (1987), p 100.

14. For a review and discussion of other forms of penetration, sometimes referred to as 'new forms of international investment', see Charles Oman, *New Forms of International Investment in Developing Countries*, Paris, OECD, 1984.

15. Yoshi Tsurumi, *op.cit.*, p 211 ff.

16. The literature on TNCs contain numerous attempts to explain why firms choose to invest abroad. The explanations usually refer to 'push' mechanisms in home countries as well as to 'pull' mechanisms in host-countries. See, for instance, Raymond Vernon, *Sovereignty at Bay. The Multinational Spread of US Enterprises*, Harmondsworth, Penguin, 1973, especially pp 71 ff, 109; Vernon, 'The Product Cycle Hypothesis in a New International Environment', *op.cit.*; J.H.Dunning, 'Explaining Changing Patterns of International Production: In Defence of the Eclectic Theory', *Oxford Bulletin of Economics and Statistics*, Vol. 41, No. 4 (1979); Sanjaya Lall, 'Monopolistic Advantages and Foreign Involvement by US Manufacturing Industry', *Oxford Economic Papers*, Vol. 32, No,

I (1980); Brooke & Remmers, *op.cit.*, Ch. 6; and F. Fröbel, J.Heindrichs & O.Kreye, *Die neue internationale Arbeitsteilung: Strukturelle Arbeitslosigkeit in den Industrielandern und die Industrialisierung der Entwicklungslandern* (The New International Division of Labour: Structural Unemployment in the Industrial Countries and Industrialisation of the Developing Countries), Hamburg, Rohwolt, 1977.

17. In this connection, I would like to raise some doubt as regards the validity of simulation analysis as a means by which to determine probable TNC responses. An analysis of this kind has been carried out by The Multinational Enterprise Unit at the Wharton School; cf. Karl P.Sauvant & F.G.Lavipour (Eds.), *Controlling Multinational Enterprises: Problems, Strategies, Counterstrategies,* Boulder, Colorado, Westview Press, 1976, Ch. 5. The authors have shown a number of scenarios to executives of American TNCs and asked how their firms would respond to similar situations. In my opinion, this method only registers the executives' conception of optimal conditions, looked at from their firms' point of view, not the conceivable reactions to deteriorating conditions in countries where the concerned TNCs have already invested. Moreover, even as respondents to hypothetical questions put forward by social scientists, these executives can serve their corporations' interests by exaggerating the negative responses to conditions that are not optimal.

18. It is within this category we find the major part of state interventions referred to in the literature as 'regulation of TNC activities' and the like. Yet, some of these regulations must be conceived of as combinations of (a) and (c) in the present enumeration. This is the case, for instance, when government support for expansion of indigenous controlled activity within a certain sector is succeeded by demands on TNCs operating within the same sector for reducing their financial participation and diversifying into other sectors.

19. For a discussion of the implications of the new forms of investment for host countries, see Charles Oman, *op.cit.,* pp 104-114.

20. The theme is elaborated in UNCTC, *Transnational Corporations and Technology Transfer: Effects and Policy Issues,* New York, 1987, Ch. I.

21. *Ibid.,* and Charles Oman, *op.cit.*

22. Charles Oman found in his study that the use of new forms varied widely from industry to industry, as well as from country to country; cf. *op.cit.*, Ch. 3.

• CHAPTER 2 •

Indian Policies Affecting Transnational Corporations

In the preceding Chapter we have presented in a simplified form our approach to the problems involved in regulating TNC activities. Moreover, we have outlined a typology of state interventions with special reference to their impact on TNC operations. While applying these conceptual frameworks, we shall now briefly discuss the Indian government's policies towards foreign private investments and transfer of technology. Within the wider frameworks, particular emphasis will be placed on policies which aim for a surplus of benefits over costs and disadvantages from operations of TNCs. We are concerned primarily with policies pursued in the 1970s and early 1980s.

The policies discussed below are analysed and evaluated primarily in terms of effectiveness, i.e., the degree to which they contribute to achieving or maintaining stated objectives. The policies are judged against two different sets of objectives. One is the set of objectives referred to in official policy declarations. Another is the set of objectives implicit in the theoretical model of internally-oriented industrial development.

In subsequent chapters the policies are also, to some extent, judged in terms of efficiency. As a concept this refers to the quantity of resources expended - or the opportunities foregone - in the effort to achieve stated objectives. The major problem involved here is the difficulty of ascertaining costs, including opportunity costs, arising from the policies pursued. Consequently, the criterion of efficiency can not be applied in a strict and quantified manner.

A third criterion which guides the analyses and assessment is responsiveness. This refers to the authorities' ability to respond to changing economic conditions and re-arrangements of priorities.

Interventions Rendering Superfluous TNC Activities

With respect to the first type of state interventions, i.e., those rendering superfluous specific TNC activities, the Indian government has not in any systematic and persistent way supported the expansion of private, indigenous business at the expense of foreign controlled companies. On the contrary, foreign enterprise has been assured non-discriminatory treatment on par with Indian enterprise within the sectors open to foreign participation.[1] Nevertheless, the government has contributed to reducing the country's dependence on TNCs by duplicating and replacing their activities through establishment and enlargement of public sector undertakings. The policy with regard to the oil industry provides a good illustration of this.

In the period just after independence, control of the oil industry in India lay overwhelmingly with private foreign companies. A few TNCs completely dominated the industry. The government attempted to change this situation through negotiations with the corporations concerning renewal of the oil refinery agreements dating back to the colonial period. But the corporations managed to pressure the government into concluding new agreements which did not, basically, affect the positions of the transnational oil corporations.[2]

Having concluded the oil refinery agreements in 1951 and 1953 respectively, the Indian government tried to persuade the corporations to use more local resources and to enter into partnerships with local business houses. Other foreign companies operating in the country generally agreed to meet such demands but, again, the majors in the oil industry, together with a number of other TNCs, managed to put themselves in exceptional positions. During the 1950s, none of the major oil corporations allowed any local common equity in their Indian refining and marketing operations, and they continued to purchase oil from sources belonging to their parent companies.

The main reason why the international oil companies were unwilling to accept local equity participation was their fear that Indian stockholders might interfere with company operations, especially by raising questions about the prices paid by indigenous refining companies to their parent corporations. This fear was related to the fundamental interest of profit maximisation in the parent company, and not in the Indian subsidiary. Accordingly, the international oil corporations preferred to import crude oil to their refining operations in India from their own sources, and they wanted that oil priced in such a way that the parent company received comparatively large profits. Further, they preferred the transportation to take place in tankers controlled by the parent companies, because this would provide them with yet another opportunity for transferring profits by means of over-invoicing.

It was in the interest of the Indian investors and the Indian government, on the other hand, to import low-cost crude oil from no matter what source, and to employ the cheapest means of transport possible. Transfer pricing in favour of the parent companies would only reduce the incomes of the Indian investors. Besides, it would reduce the taxable company incomes and affect the balance-of-payments position in India's disfavour. Consequently, local investors shared with the Indian government an interest in maximising profits in the subsidiaries.

This basic conflict of interest came out in the open in the late 1950s, when the Soviet Union offered to supply about half of India's crude oil imports at a price substantially below the one charged by the international oil companies. Moreover, the Soviet crude was offered on a barter basis. This was clearly an attractive offer for the Indian government, as the foreign exchange position of the country had deteriorated rapidly during the late 1950s, partly due to increasing demand for oil. The demand increase threatened to more than offset the saving of foreign exchange brought about by the partial shift from import of refined products to import of crude oil.

In this situation, the government tried to force a reduction in the prices paid for imported crude oil and, after having received the Soviet offer, requested the international oil companies to import and refine the Soviet crude. The companies refused. And the Indian government, it turned out, was in no position to force Soviet crude upon them, first, because it could not threaten the companies with nationalisation measures due to guarantees against such steps included in the refinery agreements of 1951 and 1953;[3] second, because neither the government nor any private Indian enterprise commanded appreciable capacity for refining and distributing the Soviet crude oil.

These facts were fully recognised by influential decision-makers in government and deliberations began with a view to expanding the tiny public sector in the oil industry. Thus, for the first time since the promulgation of the Industrial Policy Resolution in 1956, the provision contained therein that the future development of mineral oils was to be the exclusive responsibility of the state was taken seriously into consideration. The government had certainly set up public sector enterprises in the oil industry, notably the Oil and Natural Gas Commission (ONGC) in 1955, and the Indian Oil Company in 1959, but none of these enterprises played any significant role as compared to that of the major transnational oil corporations.

All this changed after the confrontation between the government and the foreign controlled oil companies. Although the latter were permitted to expand their refining capacity considerably between 1963 and 1967, they were not permitted to build or even participate in building new refineries. Instead, the government invited other foreign companies to enter into joint ventures with public agencies for the building of new refineries. Simultaneously, the distribution system set up by the Indian Oil Corporation was expanded very rapidly. As a consequence, the importance of the major transnationals steadily diminished. By 1973, the refineries in the public sector accounted for about 56 per cent of the processed crude oil, and the market share of the Indian Oil Corporation reached 60 per cent.[4]

The ultimate outcome of the confrontation over oil was an almost complete elimination of the major oil companies. In 1976, their assets were finally taken over by the government, as a result of which nearly the entire oil industry came under government control.

In the late 1970s and early 1980s, the Indian government again invited foreign oil companies to participate in the development of the industry. Oil exploration, in particular, was opened up to foreign companies. Viewed in retrospect, this policy change did not amount to a deviation from the rigorous self-reliance policies of the early 1970s. It merely constituted a modification. Foreign companies were still not permitted to attain dominance within the oil industry.

The general conclusion to be drawn from the sequence of events outlined above is that the public sector oil industry was developed partly in order to break the oligopolistic positions of TNCs within a vital sector of the economy.[5] This conformed to the overall policy of promoting internally-oriented industrial development. Furthermore, it was an expression of the government's endeavours to render superfluous specific TNC operations. In the case of the oil industry, where foreign TNCs held a dominant position and where the capital and know-how required to set up new, competing undertakings was not offered by indigenous firms, this implied a gradual reduction of foreign ownership and control by means of establishing alternative public sector refineries and distribution systems.[6]

A similar approach was applied by the Indian government in other industries, although not as systematically and persistently as in the case of the oil industry.

The general conclusion drawn from the Indian experience must, however, be viewed in a wider context. As mentioned in Chapter 1, there has been an increased willingness on the part of TNCs in general to alter their involvement from direct investment in wholly owned or majority owned subsidiaries to other forms of involvement. This major change has been particularly pronounced in the oil industry as pointed out by Charles Oman in a recent study.[7] In other words, the specific developments in India more or less coincided with dominant trends of adjustment in corporate strategies.

These strategies have undoubtedly been influenced by LDC government policies, including those of the Indian government. Nevertheless, the above observation leaves the impression that the struggle for control over equity in the oil sector was won by the Indian authorities partly because corporate strategies had changed.

Interventions Increasing the Attractiveness of India

As regards the second type of government interventions, i.e., those increasing the attractiveness of the country, the Indian government has been very active. First of all, it has invested extensively in energy, transport and communications. More than 35 per cent of all public sector outlays were allocated to these sectors during the period from 1951 to 1984, thus providing both foreign and domestic capital with greatly improved infrastructural facilities.

In this context it should be noted, however, that the primary objective was not to attract foreign capital, but rather to promote capitalist development in general.[8] Exceptions to this rule are the government-financed facilities in the export processing zones at Kandla and Santa Cruz, which were set up in 1965 and 1972 respectively.[9] These facilities were established with the express objective of attracting foreign investments and foreign technical collaborations, with a further view to augmenting exports.

In addition to increasing the attractiveness of the country in this manner, whether as a primary objective or as a consequence of other endeavours, the Indian government has consistently offered foreign enterprise a number of incentives. They include depreciation allowances; tax holidays and tax exemptions; priority access to credit, foreign exchange, import and equipment; and subsidies. The incentives have been available to foreign firms engaged in priority industries, regional development of 'backward' and 'no-industry' areas, exports, transfer of technology, and local research and development.[10]

Without entering into an analysis of the Indian government's policies in these areas, it may be safely argued that the combined result has been a general increase in the country's attractiveness.[11] This, in turn, probably has allowed the government to enact more restrictive policies towards foreign investments in other respects, without seriously affecting the inflow of capital and technology.[12]

Policies Governing Foreign Investments and Transfer of Technology

With respect to the third type of state interventions, i.e., specific regulations and restrictions which aim for a surplus of benefits over costs and disadvantages from TNC operations, the Indian authorities have developed a comprehensive and integrated system of controls. We shall confine ourselves here to an outline of the basic policies towards foreign private capital and selected aspects of the policies on transfer of technology and foreign technical collaboration.[13] Emphasis will be placed on the period after 1969.

Immediately following independence, the Indian government declared that, as a rule, the major interest in ownership and effective control should always be in Indian hands.[14] The same policy resolution, however, also stated that 'participation of foreign capital and enterprise... will be of value to the rapid industrialisation of the country'. In the years following, the latter aspect was given the strongest emphasis. The official attitude towards foreign private capital had already changed by 1949. The change was formulated explicitly by the then Prime Minister, Jawaharlal Nehru, in a Statement to Parliament.[15] By this Statement, a more flexible policy was introduced in the sense that each individual case could be dealt with on its own merits. This allowed for exceptional treatment, as in the case of the international oil companies, without any alterations in the general principles. Flexiility, of course, tended to favour the foreign companies with the largest amounts of financial and technological resources at their disposal, that is, the TNCs.

Apart from the very conspicuous concessions made by the government to the major oil corporations operating in India, the guidelines laid down in the 1948 Resolution and the Prime Minister's Statement were, in the period from 1950 to 1956, interpreted to the disadvantage of foreign capital. Private investments from abroad were welcomed only on relatively unfavourable conditions. The foreign exchange crisis in 1956-57 and pressure from various agencies representing foreign capital, however, provoked a change in attitude. The Indian government announced its willingness to accept joint ventures with majority foreign ownership, in addition to a series of tax concessions and other incentives.[16] By 1964, the government went even further in order to accommodate foreign capital, the TNCs in particular.[17]

In 1969, however, a more restrictive, selective and comprehensive approach was adopted. Thus, the government issued three illustrative lists of industries specifying the roles allotted to foreign capital in each group. The first list enumerated industries where foreign investment would be permitted with or without technical collaboration; the second list contained those where only foreign technical collaboration, and not investment, would be permitted; and the third list comprised those where no foreign participation, neither financial nor technical, would be considered necessary.[18] Besides, several foreign controlled companies came under the purview of the new Monopolies and Restrictive Trade Practices Act (MRTP Act), promulgated in 1969, and the MRTP Rules, issued in 1970.[19] Although not intended for foreign controlled companies in particular, the Act and the Rules framed thereunder affected the activities of several TNCs in the country.

More important, though, was the Foreign Exchange Regulation Act (FERA), which was promulgated in 1973. It came into force on January 1, 1974.

Section 29 of this Act referred directly to the operations of TNCs in India. According to the Section, all non-banking foreign branches and subsidiaries with foreign equity exceeding 40 per cent had to obtain permission from the Reserve Bank of India to carry on with business. They also had to obtain permission to establish new undertakings, to purchase shares in existing companies, or to acquire wholly or partly any other company. Guidelines for administering this Section of FERA were announced in December 1973, and later amended in 1976.[20]

According to these guidelines, the principal rule was that all branches of foreign companies operating in India should convert themselves into Indian companies with at least 60 per cent local equity participation. Furthermore, all subsidiaries of foreign companies should bring down the foreign equity share to 40 per cent or less. Exceptions to these rules were, however, companies exporting at least 60 per cent of their total production. Such companies could retain foreign equity shares above 40 per cent. The guidelines originally provided for only two levels of foreign equity, namely, 74 per cent and 40 per cent. Later, to provide more flexiblity, the government decided to introduce a level of 51 per cent. This level of foreign equity was permitted in cases where the company had a turnover of at least 60 per cent in core sector activities and exported at least 10 per cent of their production. The same level applied to companies exporting at least 40 per cent of their production, irrespective of the share of core sector activities. In the extreme cases of 100 per cent export-oriented units, the foreign equity share could even increase to 100 per cent.

On the basis of the reasoning behind the simplified model in Figure 2 above, it may be argued that these rules expressed the government's endeavours to force TNCs to use their superior access to global distribution and marketing systems, with a further view to improving the country's balance-of-payments position.[21]

According to another essential exception from the principal rule, companies were permitted foreign equity shares above 40 per cent if they engaged in production of items specified in a list of 19 priority industries open to foreign investment.[22] A closer scrutiny of this list shows that most of the items included were basic intermediate goods and

Indian Policies 47

means of production necessary for India's further industrial development and, at the same time, in short supply in the country.[23] Moreover, many of the products required sophisticated technology not available from indigenous sources. On the other hand, the list contained practically no consumer goods.

An interpretation of this aspect of the regulatory framework points to a desire on the part of the Indian government to force TNCs away from consumer goods industries and into capital goods industries and industries producing intermediate goods, particularly basic intermediates.[24]

After the enactment of FERA in 1974, the regulatory framework relating to TNC investments in India comprised five major acts. The most important of these were the Industries (Development and Regulation) Act of 1951 (the IDR Act); the MRTP Act of 1969; and FERA of 1973.[25] It is of some interest to compare the coverage of these acts with the primary objective of pointing out possible loopholes.

Under the provisions of the IDR Act, it is obligatory for all manufacturing companies to obtain written permission from the government for (i) establishing a new industrial undertaking; (ii) taking up the manufacture of a new article; (iii) substantially expanding the capacity of an industrial undertaking; and (iv) changing the location of an existing manufacturing unit. Exemptions from these licensing provisions have been granted to certain categories of industrial undertakings, primarily small-scale and auxiliary units.

The overall objective of industrial licensing under the IDR Act is to allocate investible resources according to priorities fixed in development plans and other policy statements. The licensing system is supposed to ensure the appropriateness of the proposed manufacturing activities.[26]

The specific objectives of the MRTP Act are to curb the concentration of economic power in private hands and to check monopolistic and restrictive trade practices. The Act covers the activities of all so-called 'dominant undertakings'. Originally, a 'dominant undertaking' was defined as a company which by itself - or along with its interconnected undertakings - produces, distributes, supplies or otherwise controls at least one-third of the total production, distribution, or supply of a commodity or service in India, or in any substantial part of the country.

Under the provisions of the Act, such 'dominant undertakings' are discriminated against in the sense that, generally, non-MRTP companies are preferred to MRTP companies when licences are issued by the government.[27]

The coverage of the IDR Act, the MRTP Act and FERA is compared in Figure 3. As can be inferred from the Figure, there are a number of options open to TNCs should they want to avoid the regulations and restrictions framed under the MRTP Act and FERA.

They can easily escape FERA's restricting influence by bringing down the directly held foreign equity share to 40 per cent - and still retain close links with TNCs abroad. In the legal sense, such companies have become Indian. In every other sense they may still be foreign controlled subsidiaries. The major point in the present context is that companies with no more than 40 per cent foreign equity, provided they are also outside the purview of the MRTP Act, can invest, expand, or diversify on the same favourable conditions as can small-scale and medium-sized Indian companies. FERA is the only piece of legislation specific to companies with foreign equity. Thus, no discrimination is permitted against foreign controlled companies in the non-FERA group.

Figure 3

An Outline of the Coverage of the IDR Act, the MRTP Act, and FERA

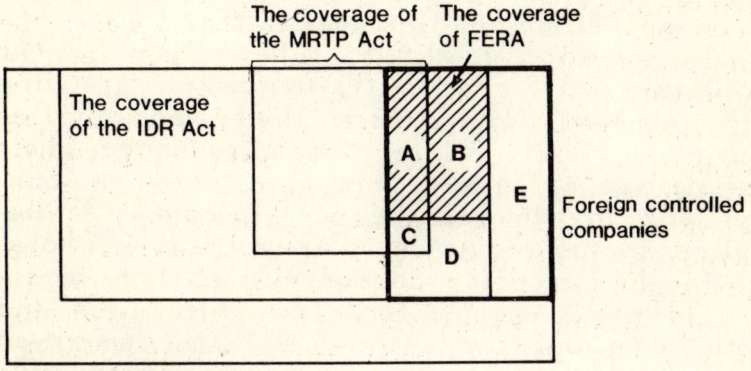

A: FERA-cum-MRTP companies.
B: FERA companies outside the purview of the MRTP Act.
C: Non-FERA companies under the purview of the MRTP Act (they may be interconnected with Indian MRTP companies or they may control more than one third of a product line).
D: Non-FERA, non-MRTP companies.
E: Smaller foreign controlled companies outside the purview of even the IDR Act.

In order to avoid registration under the MRTP Act, a TNC can spread its investment between two or more subsidiaries in India. Provided there are no formal links between these subsidiaries inside India, they do not come under the purview of the MRTP Act, even if combined they are 'dominant' according to the aforementioned definition.

It is evident from these examples that the legislation governing foreign investments in India does not cover the operations of all foreign controlled companies.[28] This must be borne in mind when analysing the implementation and effects of this legislation.

It should, furthermore, be noted that no official body has yet attempted a grouping together of foreign companies, subsidiaries or other closely related companies under their respective parents.[29] This is somewhat surprising in view of the overall objectives implicit in the regulatory framework as a whole.

In the preceding paragraphs we have focused primarily on the terms on which TNCs and other foreign companies have been permitted to invest in India. We shall now, though very briefly, review the terms on which they have been permitted to enter into technical collaboration agreements.

India initiated *control of technology transfers* just after independence. The declared policy was to promote indigenous technological research and development appropriate to the factor endowment prevailing in the country.[30] Technical collaborations with foreign companies were envisaged only when the technological know-how in question could not be obtained from any source within the country.

Not surprisingly, it proved very difficult to implement this policy. India's basis for indigenous technological research and development was extremely narrow right after independence. Besides, in their efforts to increase profitability and extend market shares, Indian companies competed to obtain not only patented technology but also the right to use well-known brand names. TNCs, on their part, were more than willing to provide the requested know-how and services, preferably in packages.

As a result of this pressure from both the Indian business community and foreign capital, the authorities actually pursued very 'liberal' policies towards import of technology and foreign collaboration agreements. 'Over-import' of foreign technology became a common feature, both in the form of import of technology already existing in the country, and in the form of import of the same technology under different brand names. At the same time, however, the authorities were persuaded by certain business groups to protect indigenous development of technological capacity. But as it turned out that this protection was given without any cost considerations, it did not necessarily imply optimal use of scarce resources.[31]

Since 1969, the terms on which foreign technical collaboration could be permitted have been made more and more specific. Besides, the policy has been integrated into the overall regulatory framework pertaining to foreign participation in India's economic development.

The long-term goal of promoting technological self-reliance has remained the same within the new framework. But the emphasis has been shifted from the question of 'indigenous availability' to that of 'the necessity for continued inflow of technology in sophisticated and high priority areas'.[32] The new policy is designed to channel imports of technology into specific areas where (i) sophisticated technology is required; (ii) critical production gaps exist; or (iii) there is a potential for increasing exports.

The new guidelines also focus on how to bring down the costs of the necessary technological imports. The Indian authorities prefer outright purchase of the technology. Only when that is not feasible, the Indian party may consider royalty payments. With respect to these, the guidelines specify both maximum payment as a percentage of the value of production and maximum duration of collaboration agreements.[33] As a corollary to this (new) cost consciousness, high priority is assigned to un-packaging of imported technology in order to ensure that only the essential constitutents of a technology package are imported.[34]

Interventions Rendering Superfluous Political Control

We have now discussed, briefly, three major types of state interventions. In addition to these, a fourth type was mentioned above, i.e., interventions with the object of rendering superfluous the state's own regulations and restrictions by supporting indigenous business.

According to official policy declarations, India's government has not supported indigenous business houses or companies with a further view to strengthening their bargaining positions vis-à-vis foreign companies. In reality, however, one of the major consequences of the operational controls applied to the private sector has been a strengthening of the monopoly and oligopoly houses.[35] This, in turn, has reduced the need for government regulations as some of the Indian business houses have acquired sufficient economic leverage and power to negotiate successfully on their own with foreign TNCs.[36] It should be noted, though, that the overwhelming majority of Indian firms are still largely dependent on state support in their dealings with large foreign companies.

Analytical Foci of the Study

In the preceding paragraphs we have included brief references to the overall effects of state interventions of the first, the second, and the fourth type mentioned earlier. It is, however, the implementation and effects of the third type of interventions that are the chief objects of this study. In particular, we intend to investigate how the policies directly affecting TNC activities have been implemented in the period since 1974.

Whereas the review of the legislation and general rules framed thereunder focused on the proclaimed policy, the study of the implementation focuses on possible discrepancies between the proclaimed policy and the policies actually pursued. This part of the study also takes into account the decision-making processes the outcome of which pertain to the operations of TNCs in India. These processes do not only involve a number of government agencies. They also comprise the very complex interrelations between the controlling agencies, the TNCs and groups representing various Indian interests, especially Indian business interests.

The investigation of the implementation processes may, in turn, be analytically separated from the effects and impacts of the decisions taken and the policies actually pursued. As regards this aspect, we intend to study how the regulatory framework, developed by 1974, has influenced the activities of TNCs in selected respects. This, the core of the present study, includes references to the impact of TNC activities on Indian economic development under the new framework as compared with the situation prior to 1974.

The strategy and objectives embodied in FERA and the whole regulatory framework established by 1974 relates to the distribution of equity and remittance of profits in the form of dividends. Therefore, it has been considered expedient to commence the analyses of effects by taking a closer look at the equity dilution process and its impact on dividend remittances out of India. Then follows a discussion of the assumptions on which the equity dilution strategy has been based. TNC responses to the new regulatory framework are investigated with respect to profit remittances, expenditure in foreign currency and exports. On this basis, the direct effects of TNC operations on India's balance of payments are studied. In particular, we have aimed at determining whether the Indian government - by means of FERA and the associated regulatory framework - has succeeded in reducing the negative and increasing the positive balance-of-payments effects of TNC activities.

Furthermore, the study seeks to identify the extent to which the Indian government has succeeded in shaping the behaviour of TNCs with regard to transfer of resources, sectoral allocation of resources and diversification of activities.

The study is concluded with a synopsis of the major findings. These findings are then discussed with a view to ascertaining critical determinants for effective control of TNC activities in less developed countries.

Notes and References

1. The closing of a number of sectors to foreign financial and/or technical participation is not primarily an expression of the type of state intervention discussed here. That kind of regulation belongs to the third category mentioned in Chapter 1.

2. A summary of these later developments is given in my *The Public Industrial Sector in India*, Aarhus, Institute of Political Science, 1980, p 71 ff. Cf. also

Michael Tanzer, *The Political Economy of International Oil and the Underdeveloped Countries*, Boston, Beacon Press, 1970; P.J.Eldridge, *The Politics of Foreign Aid in India*, London, Weidenfeld and Nicholson, 1969, Appendix 5; and Vedavalli, *Private Foreign Investment and Economic Development. A Case Study of Petroleum in India*, Cambridge, at the University Press, 1976.

3. The agreements ruled out involuntary nationalisations for a period of 25 years.

4. Over the same period, ONGC carried out a successful programme of exploration for crude oil in India, largely with assistance from the Soviet Union and Eastern European countries. The most promising oil-bearing structure discovered by the mid-1970s was the off-shore 'Bombay High'. Oil from this source started flowing to the refineries in 1976. ONGC kept 'Bombay High' for itself, allowing foreign companies to participate only in the exploration of less promising oil deposits.

5. Other major considerations behind the policy concerned the country's balance-of-payments position and the increasing domestic demand for petroleum products.

6. The nationalisation of the foreign controlled companies was not a necessary outcome of this policy. Rather, it reflected the interest of the TNCs in the sense that they probably found the attractiveness and incentives offered by India after the parallel development of public sector enterprises below the shutdown point, in terms of the model presented in Chapter 1 above. This was indicated by the oil corporations' willingness to negotiate the take-overs in the early 1970s.

7. Charles Oman, *op.cit.*, Chapter 3.

8. The Indian State's economic interventions are analysed within a broader context in my, *Staten i perifere og post-koloniale samfund: Indien og Pakistan* (The State in Peripheral and Post-colonial Societies: India and Pakistan), Aarhus, Politica, 1980, pp 1113-1158. Cf. also, *ibid.*, the English summary, p 1448 ff.

9. Cf. K.K.Subramanian & P.Mohannan Pillai, *Multinationals and Indian Export*, New Delhi, Allied Publishers, 1979, Ch. VI.

10. A summary of the incentive schemes as revised up to the mid-1970s is given in UN, ECOSOC, *National Legislation and Regulations Relating to Transnational*

Corporations, New York, 1978, Table B.4, p 120 f. A more elaborate review, including recent changes, is presented in UN Centre on Transnational Corporations, *National Legislation...* 1983, *op.cit.*, pp 56-81. Cf. also Indian Investment Centre, *Taxes and Incentives. A Guide for Investors 1979-80,* New Delhi, 1979; and Indian Investment Centre, *Investing in India. A Guide to Entrepreneurs,* New Delhi, 1987.

11. Corresponding with this contention, TNC managers interviewed in 1979 and 1983 generally referred to infrastructural facilities as one of India's prime attractions, the most important, though, being the size of the internal market. Most of the TNC-affiliated companies also admitted having benefitted greatly from the incentive schemes.

12. This proposition will be confronted with relevant empirical evidence below.

13. Detailed examinations and interpretations will be presented in connection with analyses of the implementation of policies and their effects on the Indian economy.

14. Government of India, *Industrial Policy Resolution* (1948) in: Constituent Assembly of India (Legislative), *Debates,* Vol. V, No. 1, (6th April, 1948).

15. A reprint is included in Government of India, Ministry of Finance, *India. Pocket Book of Economic Information 1968,* p 258 f.

16. Cf. Michael Kidron, *Foreign Investments in India,* London, Oxford University Press, 1965, Chs. 3-4.

17. For a brief survey of the evolution of the policy towards foreign private investment, see the Joint CTC/ESCAP Unit on Transnational Corporations, *Monitoring and Regulating Transnational Corporations in India,* Bangkok, 1980, Ch. I. A somewhat different account, analysing the evolution of policies partly as responses to pressures from foreign capital, is included in my paper, *The Indian State and the Multinational Corporations: Contribution to an Analysis of the Extra-societal Determination of State Functions,* Aarhus, Institute of Political Science, 1976.

18. The three lists are included as appendixes A.4-A.6, in: H.P.Agrawal, *Business Collaboration in India,* New Delhi, Aruna, 1979. Later, another illustrative list was added. It contained industries where foreign collaboration would not normally be permitted except on 'merits'. All these lists were replaced

in 1978 by an illustrative list of industries where no foreign collaboration, financial or technical, was considered necessary. Cf. H.P.Agrawal, *op.cit.*, p 668 ff. The press note which introduced the said list is included in: Government of India, *Guidelines for Industries,* Part I, New Delhi, 1979, Section I,pp 27-29. The list is reproduced below as Appendix II.

19. Cf. Government of India, Ministry of Law, Justice and Company Affairs, *The Monopolies and Restrictive Trade Practices Act. Rules and Regulations,* New Delhi, 1977. For a concise review, see also UNCTAD, *Control in India of Restrictive Business Practices,* (prepared by H.K.Paranjape), Geneve, 1978.

20. Cf. H.P.Agrawal, *op.cit.*,Ch. 3, and relevant appendixes; and the Joint CTC/ESCAP Unit, *Monitoring.....op.cit.*, Ch. III.

21. This was also indicated in the preamble of FERA which introduced the document as 'An Act to consolidate and amend the law regulating certain payments, dealings in foreign exchange and securities, transactions indirectly affecting foreign exchange and the import and export of currency and bullion, *for the conservation of the foreign exchange resources* of the country and *the proper utilisation* thereof in the interests of the economic development of the country'. Government of India,*The Foreign Exchange Regulation Act, 1973,* (Reprint, 1975), p 1 (emphases added).

22. The list was appended to a document introducing the government's decisions on industrial policy, dated February 2, 1973; cf. Government of India, *Guidelines for Industries,* (1979), *op.cit.*, Section II, pp 6-9. The list is reproduced below as Appendix I. Five more core sector industries were added to the list in 1982; cf. the said Appendix.

23. It may be noted in passing that, as a rule, decisions in India as to whether a product should be locally produced has not been taken on the basis of a cost analysis. The decisions have depended more on the existence of a domestic market coupled with the availability of local inputs. This was also pointed out several years ago by Vernon in: *Sovereignty at Bay, op.cit.,* p 102.

24. Extensive discussions with government officials in 1979 and 1983 supported this interpretation. The Industrial Policy Statement of 1977 and the list of 'no-collaboration' industries mentioned above in

note 17, p 38, also lend support to the said interpretation. The policy statement stressed the importance of rigorous enforcement of the FERA provisions in the consumer goods industries and proposed to freeze the production capacities of foreign controlled companies in non-priority sectors at existing levels.

25. The remaining two acts, *viz.* the Capital Issues Control Act of 1955 and the Companies Act of 1956, are not of particular interest in the present context, although some of the definitions contained in the latter are relevant to the discussion of the coverage of the above mentioned major acts. Several other acts affect the operations of the TNCs, but they are of little interest here. Some of these will, however, be considered as determining factors when we analyse various aspects of the effects brought about by government interventions. In this connection, the import and export policies pursued by the Indian government will also be taken into consideration.

26. For a detailed account, see Government of India, *Guidelines for Industries,* (1979), *op.cit.,* Section I, p 5 ff.

27. A detailed account of the MRTP Act and rules framed thereunder is given in Government of India, *The Monopolies and Restrictive Trade Practices Act, op.cit.*

28. Other examples of loopholes are presented in Nagesh Kumar, 'Regulating Multinational Monopolies in India', *Economic and Political Weekly (EPW),* May 29, 1982, p 913. Kumar also provides an illustrative account of TNCs with more than one affiliate in India, *ibid.,* pp 914-916. Cf. also S.K.Goyal, *The Impact of Foreign Subsidiaries on India's Balance of Payments,* New Delhi, Indian Institute of Public Administration, 1979, p 25. The importance of these and other loopholes in the regulatory framework has probably increased as a consequence of changes in the industrial policies effected in 1980 and 1982, respectively. Cf. H.K.Paranjape, 'New Statement of Industrial Policy', *EPW,* Sept. 20, 1980, p 1592 ff.; and Paranjape, 'The Vanishing MRTP Act: Will only the Grin Remain?', *EPW,* June 5, 1982, p 955 ff.

29. An attempt to this effect, however, has been successfully carried out by the Corporate Studies Group at the Indian Institute of Public Administration, New Delhi. Cf. Biswajit Dhar,*Foreign Controlled Companies in India: An Attempt at Identification,* New Delhi, Indian Institute of Public Administration, 1987.

30. Cf. V.P.Chitale, *Foreign Technology in India*, New Delhi, Economic and Scientific Research Foundation, 1973, p 82 ff.
31. The policies actually pursued by the Indian Government in the 1950s and 1960s are analysed by Chitale, *ibid.*
32. The quotations are from the Statement on Industrial Policy presented to Parliament on December 23, 1977; see Government of India, *Guidelines for Industries* (1979), *op.cit.*, Section I, p 22.
33. Cf. *ibid.*, p 22 ff.; and H.P.Agrawal, *op.cit.*, p 36 ff. A comparative study of the policies pursued in India, Latin America and the Philippines has been published by UNCTAD under the title, *The Implementation of Transfer of Technology Regulations: A preliminary Analysis of the Experience of Latin America, India and Philippines*, Geneva, 1980.
34. A review of India's policy for importing technology is provided in S.L.Kapur, *Policy, Procedures and Problems Regarding Import of Technology by India*, Vienna, UNIDO, 1982. See also Nagesh Kumar, 'Technology Policy in India: An Overview of its Evolution and an Assessment', in: P.R.Brahmananda and V.R. Panchamukhi (eds.), *The Development Process of the Indian Economy*, Bombay, Himalaya, 1987.
35. This was not intended according to the official policy statements. Nevertheless, the policies actually implemented generally favoured the larger business houses. This has been shown by several studies; see, for instance, S.K.Goyal, *Monopoly Capital and Public Policy*, New Delhi, Allied Publishers, 1979. I reached the same conclusion in my thesis, *Staten i perifere og post-koloniale samfund: Indien og Pakistan*, *op.cit.*, pp 1226-1276.
36. This was emphasized by representatives of some of the larger houses during discussions in 1983. When asked about the said changes, TNC representatives admitted that some of the larger houses had become much better equipped to negotiate both financial and technical collaboration agreements. The TNC representatives did not, however, attribute this change to government-sponsored growth but ascribed it to the fact that the larger Indian houses had built up more experience and expertise from previous negotiations with TNCs.

• **CHAPTER 3** •

Administration and Implementation of Indian Policies

This chapter reviews the administration of Indian policies towards foreign investments. It also discusses the implementation of FERA directives issued pursuant to Section 29, i.e., those stipulating dilution of foreign equity holdings. Other aspects of the implementation process will be dealt with in connection with analyses of the effects of India's regulatory policies in subsequent chapters.

Administration of Rules Relating to Foreign Participation

Pursuant to Section 29 of FERA, foreign controlled companies operating in India as of January 1, 1974, with more than 40 per cent non-resident interest, were required to submit applications for permission to continue their activities. The applications were to be made by August 31, 1974. All applications were processed by the Reserve Bank of India (RBI), in consultation with the FERA Committee, presided over by the Secretary of the Department of Economic Affairs. The applications were also sent for scrutiny to the Department of Science and Technology, the Directorate of Technical Development, the administrative ministry concerned, the Ministry of Commerce, and most importantly - the Department of Economic Affairs. The procedure is outlined in Figure 4.[1]

Figure 4
Outline of the Administration of Section 29 of FERA

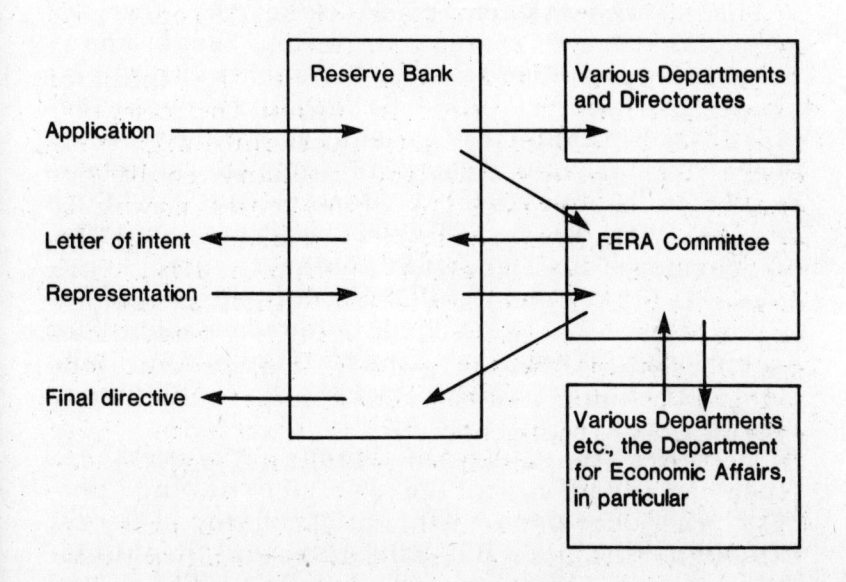

The FERA Committee examined each case thoroughly and advised the RBI whether the company in question should be permitted to carry on its business at the existing level of foreign shareholding or should be requested to dilute. In the former case, the procedure ended there with a permission issued by the RBI. In the latter case, the Bank issued a letter of intent indicating the level of permissible foreign equity. If the company was satisfied with the decision and thus willing to dilute its foreign equity accordingly, the letter of intent was converted into a final directive. If, on the other hand, the company could not acquiesce in the decision, it was offered an opportunity to present further evidence in support of its case. The application was then processed again by the RBI and the FERA Committee, now taking into consideration the contents of the company's representation.

The representation could take the form of a declaration of intent in which the company proposed to diversify activities into high priority core sectors. Or the company could declare its willingness to change the nature of operations in other respects in order to qualify for a higher level of foreign equity. Such changes had to be achieved within a specified period. The important point to note, however, is that the guidelines did provide opportunities for subsequent qualification for exceptional treatment, thus introducing both flexibility and possible delays in implementation.

It seems that, at this stage, the most influential agency in the decision-making process was the Department of Economic Affairs, although this was not stipulated in the guidelines for administering Section 29 of FERA.[2]

In deciding the conditions under which foreign controlled companies were permitted to continue their activities in India, the FERA Committee considered the guidelines issued for the implementation of Section 29. As mentioned in the previous Chapter, guidelines were originally announced in December, 1973, and later amended in 1976. The original guidelines were used mostly for disposing of cases where companies were permitted to carry on at existing levels of foreign shareholding. Most of the other cases were not settled according to the comparatively rigid rules of 1973, but according to the amended rules of 1976. Consequently, it seems appropriate to concentrate on the FERA guidelines issued in 1976.

These guidelines provided for three levels of foreign equity: 74 per cent, 51 per cent, and 40 per cent. Companies were allowed to retain foreign equity holdings above 40 per cent and up to 74 per cent, on condition that they were engaged in (i) core industries[3]; (ii) predominantly export oriented production; (iii) activities requiring sophisticated technology or specialised skills; or (iv) tea plantation activities.

If the turnover from any or all of these activities combined exceeded 75 per cent of the total turnover of the company, it was entitled to retain up to 74 per cent foreign equity. The same level applied to companies exporting more than 40 per cent of their own production or the equivalent of at least 60 per cent of their total turnover. Also tea plantation companies were permitted to retain up to 74 per cent, subject to their converting branches into foreign controlled rupee companies.

Companies exporting all of their production were allowed 100 per cent foreign equity.

If the turnover from the aforementioned activities exceeded only 60 per cent of total turnover, the company was permitted to retain up to 51 per cent foreign equity, provided it exported the equivalent of at least 10 per cent of its turnover. The same level applied to companies whose exports exceeded 40 per cent of their turnover.[4]

We shall take a closer look at the implementation of these guidelines. But before doing so, it is expedient to describe briefly the administration of the industrial licensing policy in order to acquire a general understanding of the regulatory framework of which the FERA guidelines only constituted a part.

Administration of the Industrial Approval System

The FERA guidelines applied only to foreign controlled companies with more than 40 per cent non-resident interests, and only to those operating in India as of January 1974. They did not - and do not - apply to new foreign investments, although the basic policy pursued by the Indian government in this respect since 1974 has been guided by the principles embodied in FERA. The policy has been enforced through the industrial approval system.

Another reason for looking closer at the approval and licensing system is the fact that all FERA companies, in addition to complying with the FERA directives, also had to comply with guidelines for implementation of the industrial licensing policy. Furthermore, the industrial approval system provided the government with a comprehensive arsenal of incentives and disincentives by means of which it could support its endeavours to bring down foreign equity holdings.

Companies coming under the purview of the IDR Act are required to obtain several approvals from the government.[5] These include a letter of intent which must later be converted into an industrial licence, when the company has secured other necessary approvals. After having obtained a letter of intent, the company may need the consent of the Foreign Investment Board (FIB) regarding the terms of foreign collaboration, if such collaboration is envisaged. The FIB considers whether the technology offered by the foreign party qualifies for import under the existing regulations.[6] FIB further determines permissible foreign equity levels in accordance with the stipulations contained in the FERA guidelines.

After having obtained FIB aproval, the company may have to get a capital goods clearance and foreign exchange permission, depending on the amount of imports and remittances in foreign currency envisaged in the proposal. In cases where take-overs are involved, or where capital is raised in excess of a specified limit in India, it is necessary to obtain the consent of the Controller of Capital Issues.

If the company comes under the purview of the MRTP Act, it must also secure clearance for the proposed project from the Department of Company Affairs.

With a view to streamlining these industrial approval procedures the government, in October 1973, announced the setting up of a new administrative system. An inter-ministerial committee of Secretaries, called the Project Approval Board (PAB), was established to supervise and co-ordinate the operation of the industrial approval system. Existing approval committees, such as the Licensing Committee, FIB, and the Capital Goods Committee, were made to function as sub-committees of PAB. In order to facilitate the co-ordinated and timely disposal of licensing and MRTP clearance, a joint Licensing-cum-MRTP Advisory Committee was formed. Finally, a Secretariat for Industrial Approvals (SIA) was set up to service the PAB and the other approval committees. SIA was given responsibility for receipt of composite applications, for processing them through the concerned approval committees, and for issuing the final orders of government to the applicants within prescribed time limits.[7]

The new system of industrial approvals may be outlined as in Figure 5. It should be noted that the Figure only depicts the processing of composite applications, i.e., applications for more than one type of government approvals.

Figure 5

Outline of the Industrial Approval System After 1973

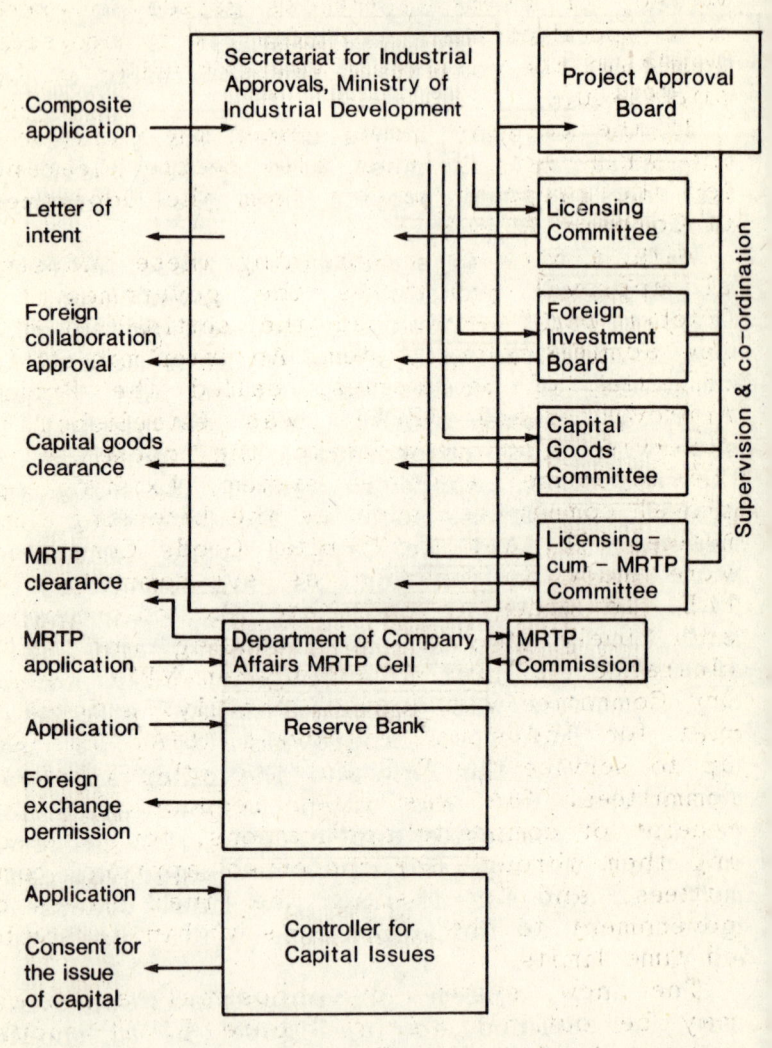

On the basis of this brief description of the administration of the industrial approval system, we can now take a closer look at the implementation of the FERA guidelines.

Implementation of FERA Provisions Relating to Foreign Equity Participation

Tables 3.1 and 3.2 present some of the salient data on the process of implementation. As can be inferred from Table 3.1, the RBI and the FERA Committee processed most of the applications within a few years. By June 1979, more than 95 per cent of the applications received had been finally disposed of. To stress the point, it may be added that cases finally disposed of amounted to more than 91 per cent as early as by the end of 1977.[8] This shows both the willingness and the ability of these institutions to make decisions in pursuance of government policy in this area.[9]

However, if we consider more closely the enforcement of decisions where equity dilution was involved, a somewhat different pattern emerges.

By June 1979, RBI had issued directions for dilution to 356 companies. Only 193, or 54 per cent of these, had carried out the dilution stipulated. A group of 99 companies were in the process of diluting. But 64 branches or foreign controlled subsidiaries had not complied. The period allowed for dilution had been extended in these cases. Even two years later, i.e., almost seven years after FERA came into force, 28 companies had not initiated the process of diluting. Not until 1982 did these companies finally receive directives issued pursuant to FERA. Some of them were permitted to retain their foreign equity at existing levels while others were directed to bring down their foreign holdings in agreement with FERA guidelines. According to RBI, all the said companies complied and initiated action on dilution of equity. According to other sources, however, at least 11 companies had not taken any steps in this direction by April 1984.[10]

Table 3.1

The Implementation of Section 29 of FERA — Selected Data

	By June 30,				
	1979	1980	1981	1982	1983
The number of applications received (since Jan. 1, 1974)	890	892	892	895	902
The number of applications disposed of	848	n.a.	865	n.a.	892
The number of directions for dilution issued (74%, 51% or 40%)	356	358[a]	358[b]	358[b]	365[d]
- of which					
carried out	193	272	300	317	332
in the process of diluting	99	38	21	41[c]	33
period allowed for dilution extended	64	37	28	0	0

a) Including 11 companies which decided to wind up.
b) Including 9 companies which decided to wind up.
c) Including 7 drug companies which were permitted to retain foreign equity at the existing levels during 1981–82.
d) Including 14 companies which later decided to wind up.

Sources: *RBI Annual Reports* 1978-79 (p 45); 1979-80 (p 40 f.); 1980-81 (p 53); 1981-82 (p 49); *RBI Bulletin (June) 1983 Supplement* (p 47); and *Economic Times*, Dec. 3, 1983.

Another indication of the delays in implementing FERA can be found in the statistics on foreign branches operating in India. According to FERA, all branches were to become Indian, i.e., register themselves in the country under the Companies Act. Nevertheless, more than 300, primarily smaller, companies

Table 3.2

The Implementation of Section 29 of FERA — The Position as on Dec 31, 1982

The number of applications received (since Jan. 1, 1974)	895
Permission to continue operations not necessary	138
Permission granted on existing basis	247
– of which approved with non-resident interest above 40% but not exceeding 74%	132
Permission granted subject to dilution and/or indianization.	362
– approval with 100% non-resident interest	1
– approval with up to 74% or 51% non-resident interest	116 (106)
– approval with 40% non-resident interest	245 (219)
Applications rejected and companies directed to wind up or to eliminate non-resident interest	97
Permission granted but companies decided to wind up	14
Companies taken over by government or merged with other companies	18
Permission granted only for limited period	9
Pending applications	10

Note: Figures in brackets refer to cases where the directives have been complied with as on Dec. 31, 1982.

Source: Indian Investment Centre, New Delhi.

were still registered as foreign branches by 1980.[11] Six years earlier, when FERA came into force, the total number of branches stood at 540.

Table 3.2 gives a more elaborate account of the decisions taken by the RBI and the FERA Committee up to the end of 1982. The Table shows that 132 companies were granted permission on the existing basis with non-resident interest above 40 per cent, while 116 companies were granted permission subject to dilution of equity to the level of 51 per cent or up to 74 per cent. One company was given consent with 100 per cent non-resident interest subject to its becoming a company registered in India. Thus, 249 foreign controlled companies were exempted from the general rule stipulating a maximum of 40 per cent non-resident interest.

The 10 pending applications were disposed of after 1982. Of these, 7 companies were directed to dilute their foreign shareholding and become non-FERA companies. The remaining 3 companies were allowed to continue with more than 40 per cent foreign equity,[12] thus increasing the total number of exemptions to 252.

There is no doubt that *most* of these companies qualified for exemption in accordance with the FERA guidelines. But, as will be shown below, there is reason to doubt that they *all* qualified.

How can the aforementioned delays in the implementation of FERA be explained? And: Can any pattern be discerned as regards the companies which did not comply with FERA regulations?

To answer the latter question first: Yes, a pattern can be identified in so far as almost all the said companies belonged to only three groups. They were either engaged in tea plantation activities or in the manufacture of drugs and pharmaceuticals, or they were affiliated with particularly large TNCs. Let us look closely at these three groups in turn and at the same time consider possible reasons for the delayed implementation of the FERA regulations.

Companies engaged in *tea plantations* qualified for special treatment ever since FERA came into force, in the sense that tea plantations were to be treated on par with 'core industries'. Thus, they were permitted to retain foreign equity participation up to 74 per cent. Branches of foreign companies were, however, required to convert themselves into Indian companies with local participation being not less than 26 per cent.

This special treatment of tea plantation companies was explained with reference to the importance of tea in India's foreign trade.[13] But it is worthy of note in this connection that approval of up to 74 per cent foreign equity participation was not subject to export of any specified share of the concerned companies' production. Consequently, it seems that the rules framed with regard to tea companies reflected extreme caution on the part of the government. The decision makers obviously felt that a more restrictive policy might prove counterproductive.[14] In particular, they feared that foreign tea companies might close down their operations in India and refuse to market Indian tea under their brand names. This, in turn, would lead to loss of substandial markets and important foreign exchange.[15]

In other words, it appears that the interests of foreign tea companies were 'built into' the Indian economy to such an extent that they could strongly influence the decision-making processes already at the policy-formulation stage. It was, therefore, not necessary for these companies to oppose the implementation of the policies provided, of course, that they could accept the special rules regarding foreign equity participation. All but a few could. Nevertheless, several tea companies refused to initiate equity dilution immediately after having received instructions to that effect from the RBI. Furthermore, a number of branches simply did not convert themselves into Indian companies for a long period. And when these companies started to comply with the FERA guidelines, they did so in slow-motion, planning dilusion processes over 3-7 years. For fear of the companies' reactions, the government responded by pursuing a policy of wait-and-see.

As regards foreign controlled companies engaged in the manufacturing of drugs and pharmaceuticals, the FERA guidelines did not provide for any preferential treatment. This was emphasized by the so-called Hathi Committee which the government had appointed in February, 1974, to go into various facets of the drugs and pharmaceutical industry in the country. In its report, submitted in 1975,[16] the Committee recommended that foreign companies in this industry should not only be directed to bring down their equity to 40 per cent forthwith, but should further reduce it progressively to 26 per cent.[17] This, as well as other major recommendations of the Hathi Committee, was not accepted by the government. Most of the recommendations were strongly opposed by foreign drug companies and their organisation in India, i.e., the Organisation of Pharmaceutical Producers of India (OPPI).[18]

During the first few years after the enactment of FERA a separate policy, disregarding the Hathi Committee's recommendations, developed. At first, the decision makers chose an interpretation of the 'core-industries' concept that favoured the foreign companies. Thus, they were allowed to retain foreign equity at levels above 40 per cent and up to 74 per cent on account of their manufacturing high priority drugs and pharmaceuticals, or on account of their employing sophisticated technology. Later, in March 1978, a new drug policy was announced. According to this, the companies could retain up to 74 per cent foreign equity only if a substantial part of their production consisted of basic intermediates and/or high technology bulk drugs.[19]

Although these new guidelines left the area for discretionary decisions wide open, there is no doubt that they expressed an intention on the government's part to tighten the control over foreign drug companies.[20]

This proved very difficult, however. It was expected that after the announcement of the new policy a number of drug companies would be directed to dilute promptly. Instead, the government appointed a committee to lay down criteria for determining what should be understood by 'high technology'. When the committee, in October 1979, submitted its report, it was clearly influenced by the companies representations and their spokesmen within government. The criteria adopted by the committee were such that most of the existing foreign drug companies could qualify for preferential treatment.[21] It is also worth noting that final decisions on the extent of foreign equity participation were to be taken in the light of representations received from the individual companies concerned. So once again the TNCs were allowed to play a prominent part in the implementation process.

They played their part so convincingly that, for another period of more than two years, they managed to prevent any significant equity dilution. Some companies brought down non-resident interest, but in most cases without giving away majority control. Two companies diluted voluntarily to 40 per cent in the late 1970s. Four companies complied with directives issued in 1978 and reduced to 40 per cent within a couple of years. But 22 companies were either permitted to retain the existing foreign holdings (9 companies) or succeeded in preventing the dilution stipulated by government (13 companies).[22] The position as on December 31, 1981, is shown in Table 3.3.

Table 3.3
The Implementation of Section 29 of FERA —The Position as on Dec 31, 1981 Regarding Pharmaceutical Companies

Permission granted subject to dilution to 40%	7
- of which in the process of diluting	3
Permission granted on existing basis	11 [a]
- approval with at least 50% non-resident interest	8
Permission granted subject to dilution where the applicants have yed to comply with government directives	13
- approval with at least 50% non-resident interest	6

a) Including 2 companies which voluntarily diluted to 40%.

Source: Economic Times Research Bureau, *Finances of Major Pharmaceutical Companies in India*, Bombay n.d. (1982), Table 5, p 14.

Why did pharmaceutical companies oppose the implementation of the FERA provisions with such vehemence and persistency? And why did the government not enforce the general rules on foreign equity participation for more than seven years?

As regards the motives behind the companies opposition, they varied somewhat from one company to another.[23] But what distinguished the pharmaceutical companies, in particular, from other foreign controlled companies was their fear of losing management control together with renouncing the majority of shareholdings. This would not normally happen, because FERA companies in general were permitted to accomplish stipulated dilutions by selling shares to a large number of Indian nationals as well as to financial institutions which would not interfere with management decisions. In this way, TNC parent companies could retain effective management control in their capacity as the largest single shareholders, even if they owned only 40 per cent or less of the equity.

This option of selling foreign owned equity, or additional equity,[24] to the general public in India was not open, however, to pharmaceutical companies according to official policy. The Hathi Committee had recommended that the dilution should not take the form of dispersed holdings of shares by a large number of Indian nationals. It would better serve the national objectives, the Committee maintained, if the shares were purchased either by public sector undertakings that were connected with the manufacture of drugs and pharmaceuticals, by public financial institutions, or by the government itself.[25]

The recommendation was never fully accepted by the government, but for several years it remained undecided whether the pharmaceutical companies would be permitted to carry out dilution by issues in favour of the general public. For as long as this was the case, the companies remained adamant in their opposition to the FERA provisions. When it became clear, by the end of 1981, that the government did not intend to enforce the Hathi Committee's recommendations on this point, several companies complied with government's directives and initiated the dilution process. Most of the larger TNCs, however, were still very cautious not to renounce their majority control.

As regards the reasons why the Indian government did not enforce the general rules on equity participation for more than seven years, they relate basically to the very powerful positions that TNCs held in the drugs and pharmaceutical industry. High-ranking government officials have explained the restraint by referring to the fact that India was very much dependent on the transnational pharmaceutical corporations for supply of several bulk drugs, drug intermediates and even essential formulations.[26] In 1976, TNC affiliated companies accounted for more than 42 per cent of the total production of bulk drugs in India and for a similar share of the total production of formulations. The decision makers in government feared that by applying the FERA provisions to these companies, they might provoke a closing down of their operations in India. Under the circumstances, this would force the country to import the drugs concerned from essentially the same corporations, but at substantially higher prices in foreign currency.

The OPPI was careful always to remind the authorities of this alternative. In a number of representations as well as in public statements, the OPPI strongly emphasized the import substitution contribution provided by foreign drug companies. The organisation also pointed out that India was only one among several promising markets for drugs and that, consequently, there was no reason to expect the pharmaceutical corporations to come to terms with too many restrictions in India.

There is no doubt that these representations involved exaggerations. They probably reflected the companies' conception of optimal conditions, rather than their conceivable reactions to the implementation of the FERA provisions.[27] Nevertheless, they strongly influenced the decision-making processes, particularly in the implementation stage. It is known that the administrative department concerned with the industry, i.e., the Chemical and Fertilizers Department, was totally opposed to applying FERA provisions on pharmaceutical companies for several years. This made it difficult for the FERA Committee to advise the RBI on the permissible foreign equity participation, because the decisions were taken on a case-by-case basis allowing the Department to exercise discretionary power.[28] The Department later changed its stand on the dilution issue by opposing a recommendation from the Department of Economic Affairs to exempt two pharmaceutical companies from dilution.[29]

Such disagreement within government undoubtedly contributed to thwarting the implementation of the FERA provisions. But the major problem continued to be the country's dependence on TNC controlled companies for the supply of bulk drugs and medicine. It was quite obvious, therefore, that should the government succeed in acquiring effective control over the companies, it had to build up parallel and substituting indigenous capacity - essentially according to the same principles as applied earlier with regard to the oil industry.[30]

This was fully recognized by influential decision-makers when, in 1978, they formulated the new policy on drugs and pharmaceuticals. Some of the objectives of the policy were to foster and encourage the growth of the Indian sector, in particular the public sector and small-scale industries, with a further view to reducing imports and the dependence on supplies from foreign companies.

In pursuance of these objectives, a number of items were reserved for the public sector and for Indian small-scale enterprises. Besides, preferential treatment was stipulated for these two sectors in the licensing policy in general. Only foreign companies engaged in the manufacture of high-technology bulk drugs or intermediates were to be treated on par with Indian controlled companies.

The agencies responsible for the implementation of the new drug policy acted cautiously at the beginning. But after the government announced its final decisions on equity dilution in December 1981, the licensing authorities applied the new criteria more rigorously, particularly when processing applications from FERA companies which had not complied with government directives. By then, the government had also initiated a comprehensive investment programme in order to build up substantial new indigenous capacity.[31] Such capacity had already been expanded during previous years in accordance with the guidelines announced in 1978. As a consequence, the position of transnational pharmaceutical corporations had been somewhat weakened.

The discrimination thus embodied in the licensing policy against FERA companies proved more effective than any other part of the regulatory framework. Seven FERA companies even went further than stipulated in the FERA provisions when, during 1984, they submitted proposals for voluntary dilution down to 40 per cent foreign equity.[32] The main objective behind these voluntary dilutions was clearly to avoid discriminatory treatment and, instead, take advantage of various benefits offered to Indian sector units in matters of licensing.[33]

Summing up this sequence of events, it is worth noting that a small group of TNCs could prevent the implementation of FERA provisions regarding equity holdings as long as they had a vital interest in doing so, and as long as they held a dominant position in strategic segments of the pharmaceutical industry. On the other hand, the same group of companies complied with government directives when the indigenous capacity for the manufacturing of relevant drugs had been expanded and when the more comprehensive industrial approval system had been employed. It is probably justified to conclude that the expanded indigenous capacity allowed the government to put more pressure on FERA companies within the pharmaceutical sector by means of withholding industrial approvals. It should be added, however, that these possibilities were not utilized optimally by the policy implementing authorities due to mutual disagreement and conflict. It should also be added that the conditions for equity dilution were at the same time changed in such a way that transnational pharmaceutical companies had no longer reasons to fear losing management control as a consequence of giving up majority control over equity.

In our investigation of the implementation of FERA provisions relating to foreign equity participation, we have now come to the third group of TNCs which did not immediately comply with the government's directives. This group comprises only a few but *very powerful corporations*. They were able to secure for themselves most 'liberal' interpretations of the FERA guidelines when the government determined permissible levels of foreign equity participation. The decisions regarding Hindustan Lever Ltd. (HL) can serve as an illustration.[34]

HLL was the largest foreign controlled company in India during the 1970s. It ranked third among all private sector companies in the country in terms of net sales.

When FERA came into force, the two parent companies, Unilever PLC, London, and Unilever NV, Rotterdam, held 85 per cent of HLL's equity.[35] As HLL concentrated overwhelmingly on soap, detergents, toiletries and vegetable oils for the Indian market, it was evident that the company would have to dilute its foreign equity holdings to 40 per cent in order to obtain the government's permission to continue its activities. The parent companies, however, proposed to the government that they should be permitted to retain a majority of the equity. Subject to this concession, HLL would be willing to plough back part of its profits into high priority industries, instead of remitting them abroad. At the same time, HLL agreed to bring down foreign equity participation to 65 per cent. This dilution was carried out in 1977.

Neither the proposal nor the said dilution satisfied the FERA Committee. But HLL managed to persuade members of the Janata cabinet formed in 1977 to defend its right to retain foreign majority, though not necessarily at the existing level. The Finance Minister, H.M. Patel, cautiously tried to obtain acceptance from Lok Sabha of a 'liberal' interpretation of the FERA provisions which would allow HLL to retain foreign majority.[36] He did not succeed, however. Consequently, after extended deliberations, HLL was ordered to reduce its foreign holdings to 40 per cent in two stages.[37]

HLL agreed to follow the government's instructions regarding the first stage and brought down the foreign shareholding to 51 per cent in 1980. But the company did not agree to dilute any further. Instead, it proposed to expand its activities in the core sectors.

In May 1982, the government approved HLL's renewed application and permitted the company to retain foreign shareholding at the 51 per cent level. The approval was given on the ground that HLL exported more than 10 per cent of its production while, at the same time, more than 60 per cent of the company's activities could be accepted as high priority activities.[38]

The authorities could reach this decision only on the basis of a very 'liberal' interpretation of what should be understood by 'core sectors' and 'high technology'. It is worth noting in this connection that 60 per cent of HLL's toiletries manufacturing was classified by government as high technology activity because the company's research and development efforts had helped it to evolve a manufacturing process for soap from minor oils, almost completely eliminating expensive imports of tallow.[39]

This import substitution aspect may be important to take into consideration when determining the permissible levels of foreign equity participation. We have to emphasize, however, that by doing so the government added a new criterion that permitted higher foreign equity – a criterion nowhere mentioned in the FERA guidelines. Besides, by taking into account the contribution to import substitution, the government did not only remove essential restrictions on foreign equity participation, it also widened the area for discretionary and administrative decisions significantly. It is well known that by leaving considerable bargaining discretion with the administrators, the policy makers at the same time actually strengthened the position of the larger TNCs. In a parliamentary system like India's, even the larger corporations are generally too weak politically to challenge basic policies of the government. But when laws and rules are framed so as to leave considerable discretionary power with the administrators, there is no doubt that larger TNCs, in particular, can influence the implementation in ways which expand their sphere of action to the very limits implied by the enabling legislation.[40]

This is illustrated in the case of HLL. From information provided by other large TNCs operating in India, it can be inferred that the treatment of HLL was an exception primarily in the sense that it became a matter of public knowledge.

Add to this that the functioning of the industrial approval system probably did not in any significant manner restrict the operations of the large FERA companies. The kind of discrimination observed in relation to most of the foreign controlled pharmaceutical companies is not found in relation to large subsidiaries in general nor in relation to subsidiaries of particularly large and powerful TNCs.[41] On the contrary, it seems that these companies are even favoured by the industrial approval system.

We shall conclude the investigation of the implementation process by taking a closer look at how the industrial licensing policy has been carried into effect vis-à-vis TNC subsidiaries.

Functioning of the Industrial Approval System

FERA and the rules framed thereunder constitute - as has been emphasized in previous paragraphs - only a part of a more comprehensive regulatory framework. Among the objectives underlying this framework, we have stressed the aim of maximizing benefits over costs from the operations of TNCs in India. As has been shown in various contexts, this implies discrimination against foreign controlled subsidiaries and branches to the extent that these companies do not operate in agreement with Indian interests and objectives. Accordingly, the regulatory framework was shaped with a view to allowing discrimination against such foreign controlled companies. Specifically, the framework allowed the government to restrict activities of companies coming under the purview of FERA and the MRTP Act.[42]

On this basis we would expect that the industrial approval system had, over the last 14 years, at least restrained the expansion of FERA- and MRTP-companies, while simultaneously favouring the expansion of Indian controlled companies, particularly those in the small-scale sector. This expectation is not confirmed, however, by available data on the functioning of the licensing system.

Most striking, perhaps, is the fact that managing directors of selected large TNC subsidiaries under the purview of FERA or the MRTP Act, or both, have not experienced any serious difficulties due to the industrial approval system. The general impression from extensive interviews in 1979 and 1983 was that they were quite satisfied with the system. As one of the directors summed up the situation, 'It takes a long time to enter the system of licensing and controls, but once you are inside, you are protected and you can make very good returns year after year'.

Managers of smaller subsidiaries, on the other hand, and those of newly established foreign controlled companies, generally expressed great dissatisfaction with the approval system. They complained about administrative 'red tape', delays, and even open discrimination with regard to issue of licences for expansion. These complaints were adduced also by managing directors belonging to companies outside the purview of FERA and the MRTP Act.

By way of comparison, managing directors of the larger TNC subsidiaries maintained that it was not a serious problem to obtain necessary clearance from government to expand production capacity, not even when it concerned products reserved primarily for non-FERA and non-MRTP companies. If an ordinary licence for expansion could not be obtained, which was often the case, there were at least three other options open, according to these managing directors.

First, the company could apply for permission to modernise machinery already installed by introducing new technology. In this case, government would normally accept a *de facto* expansion of capacity. One of the companies studied had used this procedure, in combination with the second mentioned below, to increase its capacity by over 250 per cent over the last 10 years with respect to a product reserved primarily for Indian non-MRTP companies.

Second, the company could simply install excess capacity or increase the production in excess of licensed capacity. This method has been utilized by several TNC-affiliated comnies. In a study carried out by the Corporate Studies Group at the Indian Institute of Public Administration, it was revealed that out of a total of 3,078 licences covered there were 353 cases in which the actual level of production in 1979 was in excess of the licensed capacities.[43] MRTP companies, FERA companies and a few other foreign controlled companies accounted for more than 60 per cent of these cases. The practice of attaining production far in excess of the licensed capacity, i.e., production at more than double their licensed capacities, was even more concentrated among the said companies.[44] Table 3.4 shows the percentage of excess capacity utilization for selected products. The companies listed were all covered by the FERA provisions during the period when the production in excess of licensed capacities was built up.

In July 1980, the Indian government announced its intention to recognize excess capacities already established. The regularization was confined to selected industries. At the same time, the government enjoined that violations in the future would be severely punished. Apparently, this did not in any discernible way alter the practice of producing in excess of licensed capacity or even of producing without proper industrial licences at all.[45]

Third, large TNC subsidiaries could expand their activities in India through collaboration with companies not covered by either FERA or the MRTP Act. The method has been applied in various forms. In formal agreement with government's stipulations, it has been applied by making a transfer of non-core sector activities from a FERA company to a non-FERA company controlled by the same parent corporation. By making such a transfer, the FERA company could qualify for better or perhaps even non-discriminatory treatment from government due to the relative increase in its core sector activities. Simultaneously, the

Table 3.4

Illustrative List Showing TNC-Affiliated Companies Producing More than Double Their Licensed Capacities.
(Selected Products, 1979)

Name of company	Products	Percentage of excess capacity utilization
1. Products falling under specially regulated industries		
Bayer	Pesticides/Powders	1395
Bayer	Tablets/Capsules	489
Glaxo Laboratories	Foods	111
Hindustan Lever	Milk powders	125
Hindustan Lever	Vanaspati a.o.oils	127
2. Products reserved for small-scale sector		
Guest Keen Williams	Safety pins	162
Hindustan Lever	Soaps	132
J.L.Morrison	Medicated toothpaste	115
Britannia	Biscuits/High protein food	870
3. Other products		
Bayer	Basic drugs	137
Best & Crompton	Transformer connections	136
Bochinger Knoll	Liquids for external use	185
Cynamid	Tetracycline	167
Glaxo Laboratories	Chemicals	134
Hindustan Lever	Synthetic detergents	263
May & Baker	Liquids	1616
Metal Box	R.S.Closures	308
Pfizer	Tetracycline e.a.	285
Sandoz	Liquids	410
Siemens	Rectifier cubicles e.a.	115

Source: Corporate Studies Group, *Functioning of the Industrial Licensing System. A Report*, New Delhi, Indian Institute of Public Administration, 1983, Appendices I, II, & IV.

non-FERA associate would be permitted to expand in areas closed to the FERA company. HLL employed the method in this form when, in 1983, the company initiated transfer of a substantial part of its non-core sector activities to Lipton, a non-FERA company controlled by the Unilever corporation.[46] Siemens,

General Electric Company of India, and other TNC-affiliated companies adopted similar plans in the late 1970s and early 1980s.

However, expansion through collaboration with companies outside the reach of FERA and the MRTP Act can also be carried out in violation of government provisions. This is the case, for instance, when FERA companies and MRTP companies establish small-scale units in order to avoid regulation. The Industrial Policy Resolution of 1973 specifically prohibited these companies from entering the small-scale sector. But to the categorisation of all companies with up to 40 per cent foreign equity as Indian companies in the legal sense it has been difficult for the authorities to prevent TNC-controlled firms from setting up small-scale units. In another study done by the Corporate Studies Group mentioned above, it was revealed that at least 36 affiliated companies had small-scale units in India in 1979.[47]

Other loopholes in the functioning of the industrial approval system can be identified,[48] particularly with regard to the implementation of the MRTP Rules.[49] The outline and illustrations presented, however, are sufficient for our present purpose.

On the basis of the above investigation, it appears warranted to conclude at this stage that the industrial approval system has not in any significant way restricted the expansion and activities of TNC-affiliated companies. The system may have functioned as a disincentive to some TNCs already operating in India as well as to potential investors. To the extent this has been the case, however, it appears to be the result primarily of chosen corporate strategies, rather than a necessary and optimizing response to Indian industrial licensing policies. In other words, the approval system may have 'scared away' some TNCs – possibly inflicting net costs and disadvantages on India[50] – but at the same time it has proved inefficient as a regulatory framework in relation to TNCs which have chosen to come to terms with the system.

The ineffectiveness and inefficiency of the approval system has been due partly to loopholes in the legislation governing foreign economic involvement in India.[51] Important activities are outside the purview of the acts and rules. Even a number of foreign controlled companies are totally unaffected by the special legislation. In addition to this, over the last decade, the political will has fluctuated to say the least, when it came to implementing the stipulations contained in acts and policy statements. Furthermore, lack of administrative capability has undoubtedly contributed to the ineffectiveness and inefficiency of the approval system. The administrators have not been equipped to cope with the far-reaching discretionary authority delegated to them under the acts and rules. Consequently, this aspect of the system has generally strengthened the negotiating position of large TNC-affiliated companies, particularly because of their superior technical knowledge.

Other aspects of the implementation of Indian policies will be investigated in subsequent chapters. The main focus in the following chapters, however, will be on assessing the wider impact of the policies pursued and their complex interaction with the activities of foreign as well as Indian controlled enterprises.

Notes and References

1. The description here and in subsequent paragraphs is based primarily on information provided by the Department of Economic Affairs. See also the outline of administrative procedures in UN Centre on Transnational Corporations, *National Legislation* (1983), op. cit., p 59 ff.

2. The predominance of the Department of Economic Affairs was stressed in a number of interviews with government officials and managers of TNC subsidiaries. The predominance can also be inferred from several newspaper reports on disagreement between the Department and other government agencies. In very few such cases, the conflict was resolved contrary to the expressed wishes of the Department of Economic Affairs.

3. Listed in Appendix I of the Industrial Licensing Policy Statement of 1973. The list has later been amended. See Appendix I below.

4. The guidelines are presented in detail in H.P.Agrawal, op.cit., pp 236-248.

5. Cf. p 42 above.

6. Cf. p 47 above.

7. Government of India, Press Note, dated October 31, 1973. Reproduced in Government of India, Ministry of Industry and Civil Supplies, *Guidelines for Industries 1976-77*, New Delhi, 1976, pp 82-84.

8. Fact sheet provided by the Indian Investment Centre, New Delhi.

9. Such willingness and ability can not be taken for granted. Several studies reveal that it is quite common that segments of the bureaucracy in LDCs thwart or distort official policies in the implementation phase. It is also well-known that even when government officials do want to implement proclaimed policies, they are unable to do so, either because of their administrative weakness and incompetence, or because of outside interference and economic, social or political constraints. These general observations, based on studies in India and elsewhere, have prompted us to be aware of similar discrepancies in the present context.

10. *Economic Times*, April 22, 1984.

11. S.K.Goyal, *The New International Economic Order and Transnational Corporation*, New Delhi 1982 (mimeo), p 7.

12. RBI, *Foreign Collaboration in Indian Industry. Fourth Survey Report 1985*, Bombay, RBI, 1985, p 59.
13. Over the last decade, tea has accounted for 6-8 per cent of India's foreign exchange earnings.
14. 'Counterproductive' in the sense outlined in Chapter 1, especially in relation to Figure 2.
15. This is how a high-ranking government official, who participated in formulating the FERA guidelines, explained the special treatment of tea plantation companies to me during an interview in 1979.
16. Government of India, Ministry of Petroleum and Chemicals, *Report of the Committee on Drugs and Pharmaceutical Industry*, Delhi, 1975.
17. *Ibid.*, p 98.
18. Cf. OPPI, *The Pharmaceutical Industry in India. Allegations and Facts*, Bombay, n.d.
19. Cf. Nagesh Kumar and Kamal M.Chenoy, 'Multinationals and Self-reliance. A Case Study of the Drugs and Pharmaceutical Industry', *Social Scientist*, No. 107 (April), 1982. For a brief description of the regulations pertaining to TNCs in the drugs and pharmaceutical industry, see Joint CTC/ESCAP Unit on Transnational Corporations, *Monitoring and Regulating Transnational Corporations in India*, op.cit., pp 98-105.
20. This was explained to me by senior government officials during interviews in 1979. The new policy was interpreted in the same way by, for instance, the *Financial Times*.
21. Nagesh Kumar & Kamal Chenoy, op.cit., p 18 f.
22. Economic Times Research Bureau, *Finances of Major Pharmaceutical Companies in India*, Bombay, n.d. (1982), p 14.
23. This was made clear during interviews with executives of several TNC controlled pharmaceutical companies in 1977, 1979 and 1983.
24. Stipulated dilutions could be accomplished either by disinvestment of the existing foreign equity, or by issue of additional equity to Indian nationals where the companies needed extra capital for approved expansion or diversification.
25. Government of India, *Report of the Committee on Drugs and Pharmaceutical Industry*, op.cit., p 98.
26. Based on interviews in 1979 and 1983.

Administration and Implementation

27. It is of interest to note here that none of the managers in the drugs and pharmaceutical industry with whom I discussed this matter considered the FERA provisions too restrictive. With respect to their evaluation of the Indian market's comparative importance, they all agreed that it was difficult to envisage deterioration in business opportunities to a point that would prompt them to advise closing down the operations in the country. The potential market was all too promising. However, the Indian government's restrictive price controls could easily persuade the pharmaceutical companies to discontinue manufacturing certain formulations. This was convincingly illustrated when, in 1984, at least 15 drug units stopped producing rifampicin, an advanced anti-T.B. drug, because the prices they were permitted to charge were unacceptable. Cf. *Economic Times*, August 6, 1984.

28. This was elucidated by a government official involved in the decision-making process. The views of the Chemical and Fertilizers Department are to some extent publicly known. See for instance *Economic Times*, September 10, 1981.

29. *Ibid.*

30. Cf. Chapter 2 above.

31. A concise review of recent developments in the drugs and pharmaceutical industry, including a discussion of government's role, was published as a supplement to *Commerce*, February 26, 1983: *Pharmaceutical Industry: Mid-term Plan Review*.

32. The companies were Hindustan Ciba-Geigy, Cynamid India, Merck Sharpe & Dohme, Organon India, Burroughs Wellcome, Hoechst Pharmaceuticals, and Pfizer.

33. *Economic Times*, July 17, 1984. With these expected dilutions carried out, the number of FERA companies in the pharmaceutical industry would come down to just 8.

34. HLL is called by name here because the information presented may be obtained from published sources. Information obtained through interviews, it may be reminded, is rendered in such a way that individual companies cannot be identified.

35. HLL was registered as a subsidiary of Unilever PLC, but the two parent companies actually functioned as one company.

36. *Far Eastern Economic Review*, September 22, 1978, p 102. Cf. **also** Rajan Narayan, 'The Changing Face of **Hindustan** Lever', *Business India*, July 21- August 3, **1980**, pp 32-47.
37. *Financial Times*, November 22, 1979.
38. Subrata Roy, '**The Lever-Lipton Brew**', *Business India*, July 4-17, 1983, p 50 ff.; and Ajay Kumar Rath, '**Local and Global Operations of Multinational Corporations: Unilever in India**', *Social Scientist*, Vol. 10, No. 10 (Oct. 1982).
39. **Subrata Roy**, *op.cit.*, p 51. Ajay Kumar Rath in the article mentioned in the previous note shows HHL's production falling under Appendix I industries in 1981 amounted to only 25 per cent of the company's total production. On this basis he concludes that the approval of foreign majority equity was in contradiction with FERA provisions and 'completely without any justification'. (p 34).
40. A similar conclusion could be inferred from Stanley Kochanek's classic study of the influence of foreign and Indian business upon government policies in selected respects; cf. his *Business and Politics in India*, Berkeley, University of California Press, 1974.
41. The publisised controversies between the Indian government and IBM and Coca Cola are not exceptions to this rule. Instead, they constitute extreme cases in the sense that the two companies refused to negotiate any dilution at all from the existing level of 100 per cent foreign ownership. Their position was so flagrantly in conflict with the FERA provisions that the government was left with no other alternative but to demand the closing down of the two companies' operations in India.
42. Cf. p 87 ff. above.
43. Corporate Studies Group, *Functioning of the Industrial Licensing System. A Report*, New Delhi, Indian Institute of Public Administration, 1983, p 68 ff. Cf. also S.K.Goyal, *A Preliminary Survey of Excess Industrial Capacities with the Indian Corporate Sector*, Published at the same Institute, 1980.
44. Corporate Studies Group, *Functioning...*, *op.cit.*, Appendices I, II and IV.
45. It was revealed, for instance, in December 1983, that more than 300 formulations and four bulk drugs were manufactured by pharmaceutical companies, including at least seven foreign controlled companies, without proper industrial licences. Cf. *Economic Times*, December 11, 1983.

46. Subrata Roy, *op.cit.*, p 50 ff.
47. S.K.Goyal, *The New International Economic Order and Transnational Corporations*, *op.cit.*, Table VI, pp 19-20. Cf. also the summary of a more comprehensive study in *Economic Times*, February 19, 1984.
48. As a further illustration, let me mention that capacity licensed subject to its use for export-oriented production can simply be utilized for producing for the internal market. Provided the companies concerned have been able to render probable that they have tried, in vain, to expand exports, they have normally been permitted not only to sell their production in India but also to continue producing at the higher level.
49. The MRTP Rules lack precise and operative definitions of several products. It is thus very difficult to establish the 'dominance' of particular TNC subsidiaries in the legal sense. To illustrate: Nestle's was clearly a 'dominant undertaking' in 'instant coffee' during the 1970s, but not in 'coffee' as defined in the MRTP Rules. Consequently, Nestle's escaped the MRTP regulations and restrictions.
50. To render probable this point let me recollect that representatives of smaller and medium-sized foreign firms expressed great dissatisfaction with the industrial approval system during interviews in 1979 and 1983. Some of them viewed the system as a prohibitive obstacle to further expansion in India. Consequently, they did not envisage any substantial increase in their activities. This may have implied losses to India. The said firms typically commanded sophisticated technology and specialised skills in short supply in the country. Besides, even after expansions, they would have been easier to control in accordance with government's priorities because of their size and organisation. Similar observations are probably valid for smaller and medium-sized firms that stay away from India because they expect the industrial approval system to be an insurmountable barrier. Selected executives of Danish and other foreign companies established in South East Asia, but with no affiliates or subsidiaries in India, all referred to the Indian approval system and 'red tape' as the major reasons for not having set up affiliates in the country. These executives were interviewed in 1982. A large group of Danish industrialists, assembled for a seminar on India, in February, 1988, cited the same major reasons for not having invested in India.
51. Cf. p 38 ff. above.

• CHAPTER 4 •

Effects of the Regulations on the Balance of Payments

The objective of the regulations stipulated in FERA was spelt out in the preamble to the Act. It said that the legislation aimed at regulating foreign exchange transactions with a further view to conserving the foreign exchange resources and the proper utilization thereof in the interest of the country's economic development.[1]

The means to achieve this objective did not relate primarily to remittance of profits, royalties, dividends or repatriation of capital. Such remittances by foreign companies were subject only to rules and regulations common to all companies in India.[2] Instead, the strategy adopted concerned foreign equity participation, as described in preceding chapters. More specifically, the strategy stipulated a reduction in foreign equity participation in all companies which did not qualify for exemption due to special contributions to the economic development of the country.

If we interpret this equity dilution strategy in the light of the preamble, it appears that the strategy was based on the assumption that a reduction in foreign equity participation would automatically bring about a reduction in remittances abroad. Actually, the strategy was probably based on three interrelated *assumptions*: Firstly, that TNC affiliated companies in India are making comparatively large profits; secondly, that they are in favour of largest possible remittances of their profits, and that these remittances are largely in the form of dividend; and thirdly, that profit remittances account for a substantial part of the foreign exchange utilized by TNC affiliates in India.[3]

It seems reasonable to accept the first assumption as a valid proposition. As is shown in Table 4.1, the profitability ratios for foreign controlled companies in the early 1970s were significantly higher than those for Indian controlled firms, irrespective of the exact measures used. The same pattern emerges whether we select only medium and large public limited companies or private limited companies.[4]

The other two assumptions will be discussed in subsequent paragraphs. But let us, at the moment, accept them as valid propositions and on that basis investigate the effects of the equity dilution strategy on remittances of dividends in foreign currency. These remittances were the primary target of the FERA regulations. In that sense, the proposed investigation relates directly to the intentions embodied in the Act.

Effects on the Remittance of Dividends

The amount of remittances abroad on account of dividends has varied considerably from one year to another. This is partly due to the fluctuations in the total amounts of dividends paid by all private sector companies which, in turn, reflect the varying conditions prevailing in respective branches of industry.

In order to eliminate, or at least reduce, the influence of this composite variable, it is found expedient to relate the amounts of dividends paid abroad to total dividends paid by all manufacturing companies or selected

Table 4.1

Profitability Ratios for Foreign and Indian Controlled Companies. 1971–72 and 1972–73

		537 Foreign controlled Rupee companies	2275 Indian controlled public & private limited companies
Gross profits as percentage of sales	1971–72	13.4	8.1
	1972–73	12.9	7.7
Gross profits as percentage of total capital employed	1971–72	14.7	8.8
	1972–73	14.7	8.8
Profits after tax as percentage of net worth	1971–72	13.7	7.6
	1972–73	12.6	7.6
Profits after tax less preference dividend as percentage of ordinary paid-up capital	1971–72	25.0	14.3
	1972–73	24.5	14.5
Dividends as percentage of net worth	1971–72	7.4	4.4
	1972–73	7.2	4.6
Total dividends as percentage of total paid-up capital	1971–72	13.1	7.6
	1972–73	13.6	8.2

Note: The selected 537 foreign controlled rupee companies accounted for more than 90 per cent of the total paid-up capital of all the foreign controlled rupee companies at the end of March 1973. Banking, insurance and government companies are excluded from the sample.

Source: RBI, 'Finances of Branches of Foreign Companies and Foreign Controlled Rupee Companies, 1972–73', *Reserve Bank of India Bulletin*, July 1975, Table 3.1, p 498.

groups thereof. This method does not isolate foreign equity participation and government regulations as the only independent variables influencing the size of divident remittances abroad. But the method probably leaves us with these determinants as some of the more important, thus allowing us to propose a causal relationship on the basis of an unmistakable correlation.

We expect, of course, the reduction in foreign equity participation – as stipulated in FERA – to appear as an overall decrease in dividends paid abroad as a percentage of total dividends paid. Furthermore, we expect the latter decrease to be more pronounced in the case of industries where, according to government policies, no foreign collaboration has been considered necessary.

Table 4.2 shows that, in 1975-76, i.e., before the process of equity dilution had gathered momentum, the dividends paid abroad amounted to 10.6 per cent of total dividends paid by medium and large public limited companies. There are no comparable data for earlier years,[5] but it seems probable that the average for the five-year period ending in 1975 was a few percentage points higher.[6] Nevertheless, it is at variance with our expectations, as well as with the Indian government's policies, that the share of dividends paid abroad increased to around 20 per cent in the late 1970s. After a peak in 1978-79, the share began decreasing again, but not to the level prevailing before the enactment of FERA.

A possible explanation of this unexpected development may be that foreign controlled companies, before becoming 'Indian', perhaps even while carrying out the dilution of foreign equity, decided to repatriate substantially larger profits in the form of dividends, instead of ploughing them back into their Indian operations.

This hypothesis is supported by a survey of 313 foreign controlled companies carried out by the RBI.[7] The major results concerning

Table 4.2

Dividends Paid Abroad as a Percentage of Total Dividends Paid by Medium and Large Companies, 1975-76 to 1980-81

	No. of companies	Total dividends paid (lakhs of Rs.)	Dividends paid abroad (lakhs of Rs.)	Dividends paid abroad as a percentage of total dividends
1975-76	1720	183,75	19,52	10.6
1976-77	1720	209,34	36,85	17.6
1977-78	1720	227,62	44,02	19.3
1978-79	1720	259,04	52,03	20.1
1979-80	1720	287,11	46,78	16.3
1980-81	1720	317,24	44,55	14.0
1980-81	1651	337,66	49,09	14.5
1981-82	1651	365,33	52,33	14.3
1982-83	1651	376,16	64,27	17.1

Note: Insurance, banking and government companies are excluded from this study.

Sources: Calculated on the basis of RBI, 'Finances of Medium and Large Public Limited Companies, 1977-78' *Reserve Bank of India Bulletin*, May 1980, Tables 2 & 14; and RBI, 'Finances of Medium and Large Public Limited Companies, 1980-81', *Reserve Bank of India Bulletin*, July 1983, Tables 2 & 13; and RBI, 'Finances of Medium and Large Public Limited Companies, 1982-83, *Reserve Bank of India Bulletin*, February 1985, Tables 2 & 10.

dividend remittances are summarized here in Table 4.3. It reveals that remittances from the sample of foreign controlled companies increased from Rs. 16 crores in 1975-76 to Rs. 51 crores in 1978-79. In the following years they declined to Rs. 44 crores and 41 crores, respectively. The share of dividend remittances in total dividends reflected the same pattern

Table 4.3

Dividends Paid Abroad as a Percentage of Total Dividends Paid by 313 Foreign Controlled Rupee Companies, 1975-76 to 1980-81

	Total dividends paid (lakhs of Rs.)	Dividends paid abroad (lakhs of Rs.)	Dividends paid abroad as a percentage of total dividends
1975 - 76	72,63	16,26	22.4
1976 - 77	90,11	N.A.	-
1977 - 78	93,29	42,35	45.4
1978 - 79	114,70	50,58	44.1
1979 - 80	121,92	44,14	36.2
1980 - 81	123,91	40,97	33.2

Source: Calculated on the basis of data presented in RBI, 'Finances of Foreign Controlled Rupee Companies and Branches of Foreign Companies, 1975-76 to 1980-81', *Reserve Bank of India Bulletin*, August 1984, Statement 6, p 315, Statement 17, p 343, and p 294.

as shown with reference to the corporate sector as a whole in Table 4.2. Thus, the share of dividends remitted abroad by foreign controlled companies went up from 22 per cent of total dividends in 1975-76 to more than 45 per cent in 1977-78. Subsequently, the share declined, but it remained at a higher level than in the mid-1970s.

Irrespective of the precise causal relationships, there is probably no doubt that the Indian government's equity dilution policy contributed, in the short run, to unintended effects as regards outflow of foreign currency in the form of dividends. It remains to be ascertained how the policy will influence the payment of dividends in the long run. The outcome will, to some extent, depend on the distribution of foreign held equity between various branches of industry, characterized by dissimilar conditions for expansion and making of profits.

This is one reason for taking a closer look at the payment of dividends in selected branches of industry. Another is to find out whether the shares of dividends paid abroad from various industries have formed a pattern in agreement with government policies. If so, we should be able to discern a decline at least with respect to those branches of industry, where the government has not envisaged any new foreign financial participation. These are also the areas where companies already engaged did not, as such, qualify for exemption from the equity dilution rules.

Table 4.4 presents data on dividends paid abroad by medium and large private sector manufacturing companies, classified according to industry. Furthermore, the industries listed are divided into two major groups. The first comprises industries processing and manufacturing primarily items for which no foreign financial collaboration has been deemed necessary since 1969.[8] The second group consists of selected, relatively important industries open to new foreign investments on a joint-venture basis.

Certain reservations must be made with regard to the division of industries in the Table. The most important is that, government policies have not precluded expansion of existing joint ventures in group A industries. Besides, they have not precluded composite schemes of manufacturing where the production of otherwise reserved items has been envisaged along with major items for the manufacture of which foreign financial participation has been permitted. Finally, some of the products manufactured by 'other industries' in the Table are included in the list of items for which no foreign financial collaboration has been deemed necessary

In spite of these and other reservations, we believe that the data presented can be used as valid and reliable indicators of the effects studied here, provided the variations are interpreted conservatively and with great caution.

The most conspicuous variations in Table 4.4 correspond with the general pattern identified on the basis of Table 4.2, i.e., an increase in the share of dividends paid abroad in the years subsequent to the enactment of FERA. This increase was followed by a pronounced decline, again around 1980. Very few industries do not conform to this pattern.

If we compare the dividends paid abroad by group A industries in the early 1980s with those paid during 1975-1978, it is surprising that no significant decline can be discerned. If we use the weighted averages for two three-year periods in order to avoid short-term fluctuations, it is even more surprising that substantial declines can be identified in only a few industries. Furthermore, it is worthy of note that in 'other food products' and 'tobacco', where a significant decline did occur, the level of dividend remittances abroad remained high. It is also worth mentioning that in 'tobacco', the share of dividends paid abroad went up again - and significantly so - in 1982-83.

As regards industries in group B, it is interesting to note that the aggregate data for 'engineering' and 'chemicals' - combined accounting for more than 51 per cent of total dividends paid during 1980-81 - show neither decline nor substantial increase from the first three-year period to the second. The aggre-

Table 4.4
Dividends Paid Abroad by Medium and Large Companies – Industry-wise
(1975–1981)

Industry	Total dividends paid 1980-81 (Lakhs of Rs.)	No. of companies 1978-81	Dividends paid abroad as a percentage of total dividends				Weighted average		
			1978-79	1979-80	1980-81	1975-76/ 1977-78	1978-79/ 1980-81	1981-82	1982-83

A.

Industries processing and manufacturing primarily items for which no foreign financial collaboration has been considered necessary

Sugar	3,61	57	–	–	1.1	0.8	0.4	–	–
Other food products	3,94	31	58.9	29.4	22.6	42.2	35.6	N.A.	N.A.
Tobacco	6,26	8	22.1	24.5	22.2	33.0	22.9	21.6	55.1
Cotton textiles	28,99	238	6.0	2.4	2.8	4.6	3.6	3.5	3.4
Jute textiles	1,18	31	–	–	–	–	–	–	–
Silk & rayon textiles	7,88	13	2.3	1.5	2.5	2.7	2.1	–	–
Woollen textiles	1,22	10	–	–	–	2.8	–	–	–
Breweries & distilleries	1,64	10	–	–	–	–	–	–	–
Man-made fibres	12,69	13	9.4	8.9	8.5	12.9	8.9	N.A.	N.A.
Paints, varnishes, etc.	1,61	15	24.8	24.3	11.8	18.0	19.9	N.A.	N.A.
Dyes & dyestuffs	5,39	10	13.8	14.1	14.3	14.2	14.0	N.A.	N.A.
Cement	5,96	15	3.5	3.1	4.0	1.8	3.5	4.4	–
Pottery, china, etc.	1,80	19	–	–	–	–	–	–	–
Paper and paper products	9,83	41	4.2	4.1	4.9	3.8	4.4	4.5	4.9
Glass & glassware	1,64	12	14.6	17.5	20.1	14.4	17.4	N.A.	N.A.

B. Other industries

Engineering – total	93,10	461	20.4	19.6	18.5	19.3	19.4	17.6	19.3
– of which									
Motor vehicles	21,12	42	14.0	14.8	15.5	21.7	14.9	13.9	13.0
Electrical machinery	28,16	112	26.0	24.7	24.2	23.3	24.9	24.6	26.3
Other machinery	25,96	149	21.3	20.4	17.4	14.3	19.5	16.3	19.3
Foundries & engineering workshops	6,67	72	11.7	8.9	6.4	8.3	8.5	8.4	5.5
Metal products	10,12	67	19.7	17.9	19.7	25.7	19.1	17.5	25.7
Aluminium	6,17	3	2.2	47.2	21.2	33.7	21.5	45.5	32.7
Chemicals – total	70,39	204	38.3	24.3	19.8	25.7	27.4	15.8	24.8
– of which									
Chemical fertilizers	10,42	13	89.8	22.6	21.5	27.9	48.3	21.9	12.9
Basic industrial chemicals	11,78	42	14.3	16.3	18.1	20.0	20.6	9.9	13.3
Medicines & pharmaceuticals	11,57	52	42.9	43.1	46.2	32.9	44.0	41.5	37.6
Rubber & rubber products	7,20	20	30.3	17.4	22.8	31.0	22.5	22.9	19.4

Note: Only selected, relatively important manufacturing industries are included in the table.

Unfortunately, the RBI has changed the composition of tables leaving out a number of industries which were included in the breakdowns for the 1970s.

Sources: Calculated on the basis of information provided by RBI in the Bulletins referred to as sources for Table 4.2.

gated figures conceal some variation in individual industries, but still no clear pattern reflecting official policies can be identified. The constantly high share of dividends remitted abroad by the pharmaceutical industry is even at variance with government policies.

Add to this the fact that companies engaged in agriculture, plantations and manufacturing activities not listed in Table 4.4 did not show any reduced propensity to remit dividends abroad.[9] On the other hand, the relatively important tea plantation companies increased the share of dividends paid abroad from 17 per cent in 1975-76 to more than 32 per cent in 1980-81.

On this basis, it seems reasonably safe to conclude that one of the primary objectives of FERA had not yet, by the early 1980s, been realized. The drain on foreign exchange resources on account of dividend remittances had not, after eight years of equity dilution, been brought down to a level below the one prevailing in 1975-76.

This does not imply, though, that FERA has remained ineffective in this respect even after 1983. Actually, we have reason to assume that the general tendency of decline initiated during 1977-79 in most industries has continued in recent years, thus reflecting a delayed reaction and adjustment to government regulations. A final conclusion with regard to this causal relationship must, however, await the processing of data relating to the three-year period ending in 1987.

Dividend and Other Remittances

No matter how the FERA regulations have affected the drain on foreign exchange resources on account of dividend remittances, it remains to be investigated whether these remittances constituted any substantial part of total remittances abroad. In the preceding discussion we assumed that TNC-affiliated companies in India were in favour of largest possible remittances of their profits and that these were largely in the form of dividends. We also assumed that profit remittances accounted for a substantial part of the foreign exchange utilized by TNC affiliates in India. These assumptions may be questioned, however.

The approach of TNC-affiliated companies to profit remittances is shaped primarily by the management's perceptions of future business opportunities.[10] If the prospects for their operations are perceived as bleak they may favour the largest possible remittances at the earliest. If, on the other hand, the managements hold the view that India offers a promising future for their operations, the policy would be to expand their production base in order to create a better potential for future growth. This does not rule out substantial remittances of profits during periods when these are exceptionally high, but it precludes that TNCs would favour the largest possible remittances if this approach would prevent the building up of an expanded production base.

The attitude of TNC managers in India during the late 1970s and early 1980s with regard to future business prospects was overwhelmingly optimistic. This was brought out very clearly during interviews with several top managers and other representatives of foreign companies. Among those interviewed, only one manager – belonging to a comparatively small TNC subsidiary – held the view that India did not offer future promising business opportunities, mainly because of increasing labour problems and administrative 'red tape'. All other managers emphasized the importance of expanding and diversifying the production base in order to meet expected significant increases in demand. Similar opinions have been put forward in public by a large number of foreign business representatives.[11]

The actual behaviour of most of the TNC-affiliated companies in India has been in keeping with these perceptions and expectations. Their assets have been growing fast, appreciably faster than those of comparable Indian companies.[12] Besides, most TNCs in India have accumulated large reserves against which they have issued bonus shares quite extensively, especially before the dilution of equity.[13]

These data suggest that TNCs have not, as a rule, been in favour of maximizing their profit remittances abroad.

As regards the assumption that profit remittances have been largely in the form of dividends, this is a valid proposition if by 'profit' is understood the accounting concept.[14] Then it is evident that profit remittances have been chiefly in the form of dividends. If, however, by the term 'profit' we understand the economic concept of profit or benefit, the importance of dividend remittances is reduced considerably.[15] The accounting profits that appear in the balance sheets of the companies may be very different from the direct and indirect economic benefits accruing to the companies from the operations concerned. This is true, in particular, for TNCs because they can apply transfer pricing not only to adjust *what* accounting profit is declared *where*, but also to transfer resources and economic surplus from one subsidiary to another or from a subsidiary to the parent company.

The extent to which TNCs operating in India indulge in transfer pricing is not known. In view of the fact that the possibilities and the incentives are many and varied it seems obvious, however, that they would - in accordance with their global economic interests - resort to this practice as a supplementary means of transferring economic surplus out of India.

Add to this the FERA objective of conserving foreign exchange resources and the proper utilization thereof, irrespective of the specific type of outward flow. It then becomes apparent that remittances of accounting profits should be analysed in connection with other resource flows which might involve transfers of economic surplus. More specifically, it becomes of interest to consider dividend and other remittances in relation to the total expenditures of TNC affiliates in foreign currency.

Effects on Expenditure in Foreign Currency

The Reserve Bank of India has carried out a comprehensive study of 313 foreign controlled companies in the processing and manufacturing industries. From this study we have extracted pertinent data on the companies' expenditure in foreign currency. The data are presented here in Table 4.5.

It is evident from the Table that remittances of dividends account for only a minor share of foreign exchange utilization. Even at its highest level, in 1977-78 (not shown in the Table), it did not exceed 13 per cent.[16] Imports account for the bulk of the foreign exchange utilized by foreign controlled companies.[17] A closer scrutiny of the data shows that the imports consisted chiefly of raw materials and components.

Irrespective of the precise relative importance of dividends and other remittances, it remains obvious that the FERA strategy of equity dilution cannot be the only, nor even the main instrument for achieving a substan-

Table 4.5

Foreign Exchange Utilization by 313 Foreign Controlled Rupee Companies, 1975-76, 1979-80 and 1980-81

	1975-76 Rs.lakhs	%	1979-80 Rs.lakhs	%	1980-81 Rs.lakhs	%
Imports	193,21	82.5	390,59	84.6	458,22	86.4
Other expenditure in foreign currency	41,13	17.6	71,05	15.4	72,36	13.6
Of which:						
– Royalty	4,16	1.8	3,33	0.7	4,41	0.8
– Technical fees	3,89	1.7	5,79	1.3	6,63	1.3
– Interest	5,44	2.3	2,53	0.6	2,53	0.5
– Dividends remitted	16,26	6.9	44,14	9.6	40,97	7.7
Total outgo in foreign currency	234,34	100.1	461,64	100.0	530,58	100.0

Sources: Calculated on the basis of RBI, 'Finances of Foreign Controlled Rupee Companies and Branches of Foreign Companies, 1975-76 to 1980-81', *Reserve Bank of India Bulletin*, August 1984, Statement 17, pp 343-348, and Statement 18, p 345.

tial reduction in the total utilization of foreign exchange by TNCs in India.[18]

So far, we have focused exclusively on transactions of TNC-affiliated companies. Considering, however, that FERA aimed at regulating foreign exchange transactions in general, including those of Indian controlled companies, it is of interest to widen the perspective to include the whole private corporate sector. How has FERA influenced the size and pattern of the private sector's utilization of foreign exchange? Or, since we cannot isolate the influence of FERA, how has the regulatory framework comprising FERA and various import controls affected the said size and pattern.

As may be inferred from Tables 4.6 and 4.7, the remittances on account of dividend varied appreciably during the decade after 1969. The absolute as well as the relative size of remittances on this account remained at a high level during the first five-year period. After that, a significant drop followed in 1974-75. Subsequent years again showed an increase - in keeping with the pattern identified earlier.[19]

Table 4.6

Remittances Made Abroad by Private Sector Companies, 1969-70 to 1978-79

Rs. lakhs

	Profits	Dividends	Royalties	Technical Fees	Interest	Total
1969-70	12,72	31,41	5,80	13,05	9,28	72,26
1970-71	13,12	43,48	5,23	20,63	12,80	95,26
1971-72	9,94	38,87	5,86	13,90	12,13	80,70
1972-73	15,54	39,08	7,33	11,33	15,60	88,88
1973-74	21,91	37,51	6,21	14,08	16,27	95,98
1974-75	7,19	18,46	8,46	12,56	36,70	83,37
1975-76	20,36	24,84	10,49	25,66	24,65	106,00
1976-77	19,39	48,47	15,88	37,80	25,11	146,65
1977-78	10,13	68,01	19,50	28,14	22,70	148,48
1978-79	10,24	54,35	12,65	55,52	31,44	164,20
1979-80	14,07	50,92	9,53	43,97	25,22	144,01
1980-81	12,10	55,92	8,88	104,93	22,32	204,15
1981-82	12,16	58,92	15,99	270,70	41,08	398,85
1982-83	19,12	70,31	39,72	258,58	80,23	467,96
1983-84	20,00	62,11	27,60	314,89	81,51	506,11

Source: Indian Investment Centre, New Delhi.

Fluctuations continued after 1979. But in relative terms dividend remittances decreased significantly when, in keeping with FERA stipulations, the dilutions began to take effect. As shown in Table 4.7, dividend remittances accounted for only around 15 per cent in the early 1980s – as compared to more than 40 per cent in 1970-71.

This relative decrease was explained primarily by a considerable increase in technical payments, i.e., payments in respect of royalties, technical know-how, management services,

Table 4.7

Remittances Made Abroad by Private Sector Companies, 1969-70 to 1978-79

Percentage Distribution

	Profits	Dividends	Royalties	Technical Fees	Interest	Total
1969-70	17.6	43.5	8.0	18.1	12.8	100.0
1970-71	13.8	45.6	5.5	21.7	13.4	100.0
1971-72	12.3	48.2	7.3	17.2	15.0	100.0
1972-73	17.5	43.9	8.3	12.8	17.5	100.0
1973-74	22.8	39.1	6.5	14.7	16.9	100.0
1974-75	8.6	22.1	10.2	15.1	44.0	100.0
1975-76	19.2	23.4	9.9	24.2	23.3	100.0
1976-77	13.2	33.1	10.8	25.8	17.1	100.0
1977-78	6.8	45.8	13.1	19.0	15.3	100.0
1978-79	6.2	33.1	7.7	33.8	19.2	100.0
1979-80	10.0	35.4	6.6	30.5	17.5	100.0
1980-81	5.9	27.4	4.3	51.4	10.9	99.9
1981-82	3.0	14.8	4.0	67.9	10.3	100.0
1982-83	4.1	15.0	8.5	55.3	17.1	100.0
1983-84	4.0	12.3	5.5	62.2	16.1	100.1

Source: Table 4.6.

etc. Tables 4.6 and 4.7 reveal an unmistakable rising trend in technical payments since 1974.[20] As a percentage of total payments abroad, those on account of technical fees alone rose from around 20 per cent in the mid-1970s to more than 55 per cent in the early 1980s.

The modest magnitude of technical payments during the Fourth Five Year Plan period (1969-1974) was caused partly by stricter regulations for royalty payments enforced by the government in 1968. Subsequently, resort to lumpsum payments for technology, modifications of the regulations and special facilities for various industries, all paved the way for a significant increase in total technical payments after 1974. The tendency was accentuated further by shifts in the pattern of foreign investment and collaboration from low to high technology areas. Other contributory factors include the generally higher preference on the part of TNCs for so-called new forms of investment involving no or only minority financial participation, but considerable technical collaboration. It seems highly probable that for such companies technical payments have, to a great extent, served as means of remitting profits. In agreement with this proposition, earlier studies have indicated that foreign minority-owned firms have showed a significantly higher propensity than foreign majority-owned companies to remit 'profits' in the form of technical payments.[21] The equity dilution process, started by the FERA regulations, directly affected the remittance pattern, in the sense that they brought about an increase in the relative share of foreign minority-owned companies and, consequently, an increase in the relative share of technical payments.

As pointed out above, remittances on account of dividends, technical payments, etc., only constitute a minor share of total foreign exchange utilization by the private corporate sector. The bulk of the outgo of foreign currency is on account of imports. This is the case not only with regard to foreign controlled enterprise but also with regard to Indian companies.

Table 4.8 presents aggregate data based on the RBI surveys of medium and large public limited, non-financial and non-government companies. The Table shows similar fluctuations, during the 1970s, to those identified earlier with respect to dividend remittances. There are some conspicuous fluctuations in the payment of dividends, technical fees and other remittances, particularly in 1976-77 and 1982-83. But basically, it is difficult to discern any substantial changes in the pattern after the new regulatory framework came into effect.

In order to investigate whether the aggregated data conceal appreciable changes within particular industrial groups we have computed comparable data for engineering industries, chemical industries and selected consumer goods industries separately.[22] These disaggregated figures show basically the same pattern as depicted in Table 4.8, with chemical industries only slightly deviating in the sense that expenditure on account of imports tended to increase distinctly more after 1979.[23] This was probably partly due to the rise in oil prices.

The data analysed here do not permit a conclusion to the effect that the FERA regulations substantially changed the pattern of foreign exchange utilisation by the private corporate sector during the period studied. This could not be expected, perhaps, in view of the conclusion reached earlier with respect to dividend remittances.[24] At any rate, the pre-

Table 4.8 The Structure of Expenditure in Foreign Currency by Medium and Large Companies, 1975-76 to 1982-1983.

	1975-76	1976-77	1977-78	1978-79	1979-80	1980-81	1981-82	1982-83
Imports	86.6	83.8	88.0	85.2	87.2	88.0	87.8	83.0
- of which								
Raw materials	66.1	63.9	71.3	66.2	66.5	62.9	62.3	59.2
Capital goods	9.8	9.3	7.5	8.5	7.8	12.3	13.5	13.6
Stores and spares and others	10.7	10.6	9.2	10.6	12.9	12.7	12.0	10.2
Remittances								
- of which								
Dividends	3.2	5.4	4.5	4.7	3.4	2.9	2.5	2.8
Royalty	1.4	1.4	1.0	0.7	0.7	0.7	0.8	0.8
Technical fees and other fees	1.4	2.9	0.6	0.9	0.8	0.9	0.5	0.8
Other remittances	7.4	6.5	5.9	8.5	7.9	7.6	8.4	12.6
Total	100.0	100.0	100.0	100.0	100.0	100.0	100.0	100.0
Total expenditure (Rs. lakhs)	601,31	681,40	978,64	1110,30	1373,81	1560,62	2109,61	2287,35

Note: Group III-industries include edible oils, sugar, other food products, tobacco, cotton textiles, jute textiles, silk and rayon textiles, woolen textiles, breweries and distilleries. Only some of these industries could be included in the figures for 1981-82 and 1982-83 due to changes in the RBI statements.

Sources: As for Table 4.2.

ceding analysis only confirms that FERA had little intended impact on profit remittances before the mid-1980s and that FERA probably did not affect the relative importance of these remittances.

It remains to be investigated, however, whether FERA and other elements of the new regulatory framework brought about a decline in remittances relative to total sales of the private corporate sector. Such a decline would be in keeping with overall policy objectives of increasing self-reliance and reducing the costs of production in foreign currency.

Remittances of the private corporate sector for the eight-year period after 1975 are summarized in Table 4.9. The figures for dividend remittances as a percentage of total sales depict the familiar pattern of increase over the first four years, followed by a decline. Other remittances, however, rose from a level of around 0.5 per cent during the first three years to a level above 0.6 per cent during the last three years. Total remittances thus showed no decline in relation to sales. Actually, they increased towards the end of the period covered in the Table.

The policy objectives referred to above concerning self-reliance and costs of production in foreign currency also implied endeavours to bring down the share of import in total income, sales and consumption. As can be inferred from Table 4.9, these endeavours did not succeed with regard to the private corporate sector. On the contrary, total imports as a percentage of sales rose from below 4 per cent to around 6 per cent over the period investigated.

It is worthy of note that, concealed behind these aggregated figures for all medium and large private sector companies, there is a marked difference between Indian and foreign con-

Table 4.9

The Private Corporate Sector's Utilisation of Foreign Currency and Total Sales, 1975-76 to 1980-81

	Sales		Total imports		Dividends paid abroad		Other remittances	
	Rs.lakhs	%	Rs.lakhs	%	Rs.lakhs	%	Rs.lakhs	%
1975-76	13171,14	100.00	520,72	3.95	19,52	0.15	61,09	0.46
1976-77	14581,00	100.00	520,72	3.91	36,85	0.25	73,83	0.51
1977-78	15949,00	100.00	860,77	5.40	44,02	0.28	73,86	0.46
1978-79	17563,89	100.00	946,07	5.39	52,03	0.30	112,21	0.64
1979-80	20267,93	100.00	1197,98	5.91	46,78	0.23	129,05	0.64
1980-81	23736,07	100.00	1373,10	5.78	44,55	0.19	142,97	0.60
1981-82	29284,85	100.00	1852,96	6.33	52,33	0.18	204,32	0.70
1982-83	31837,00	100.00	1897,58	5.96	64,27	0.21	325,52	1,03

Sources: As for Table 4.2.

trolled companies. It is quite natural that foreign controlled companies remit comparatively higher sums in foreign currency on account of dividends, technical payments, etc. What is interesting here is that they also import substantially more than their Indian counterparts in proportion to total income, sales and consumption.

As an illustration of this 'higher propensity to import' we have shown, in Table 4.10, the values of imported raw materials, components, stores and spares as percentages of total values of those consumed by 1353 companies. During the period studied, foreign controlled companies as a whole were characterized by a distinctly higher import content than Indian companies included in the sample. The ratios of imported to total raw materials, components, etc., declined in 1978-79, but only to start climbing again in subsequent years.[25]

Other studies have revealed the same general tendency for foreign controlled companies to import relatively more than Indian companies. K.K.Subramanian and P.Mohanan Pillai observed in their study of 60 engineering companies that the average import intensity was the highest among foreign subsidiaries in all product lines, with the exception of electronics, and the lowest among Indian firms with no or low foreign association. Actually, it was found that the average import intensity varied with the degree of foreign association, i.e., the higher the foreign association, the higher the import content.[26] Similar patterns were revealed with respect to the pharmaceuticals industry and the dyestuffs and intermediates industry, although the highest import intensity in these cases were found among joint ventures with foreign minority ownership. Majority-owned foreign companies came in as close seconds.[27]

Table 4.10

Imported to Total Raw Materials, Components, Stores and Spares Consumed, 1975-76 to 1977-78

Percentages

	1975-76	1976-77	1977-78
1353 Companies	10.2	11.0	14.5
Of which:			
276 Foreign controlled rupee companies	12.8	14.0	15.5
1077 Indian companies	9.1	9.7	14.1

Note: The study covers 1353 medium and large companies in the processing and manufacturing industry. The companies, included in the RBI study of 1720 operating companies with paid-up capital of Rs 5 lakhs or above, accounted for about 96 per cent of the outgo in foreign currency of the 1720 companies.

Sources: RBI, 'Foreign Exchange Earnings and Outgo by Medium and Large Processing and Manufacturing Companies; 1975-76 to 1977-78', *Reserve Bank of India Bulletin*, July 1981, Table 1, p 562, and Statement 2, p 580.

In addition to their generally higher propensity to import, as compared to Indian companies, foreign controlled firms have also shown an *increasing* preference for imports. This is illustrated in Table 4.11. The data reveal a disturbing tendency among foreign controlled companies to import increasingly higher proportions of raw materials, components, stores and spares consumed.

The same trend is displayed in the RBI's fourth survey report on foreign collaboration in Indian industry.[28]

Table 4.11

Imported to Total Raw Materials, Components, Stores and Spares Consumed by 313 Foreign Controlled Rupee Companies, 1975-76 to 1980-81

Percentages

	1975-76	1976-77	1977-78	1978-79	1979-80	1980-81
Raw materials & components	12.3	14.2	14.7	14.0	15.3	16.4
Stores and spares	4.0	5.4	5.7	6.4	9.6	12.9
Total	11.5	13.4	13.9	13.3	14.8	16.1

Source: Calculated on the basis of RBI, 'Finances of Foreign Controlled Rupee Companies and Branches of Foreign Companies, 1975-76 to 1980-81', *Reserve Bank of India Bulletin*, August 1984, Statement 15, pp 339-341.

Effects on the Balance of Payments

The fact that the import content for companies with close foreign connections tend to be higher than that for other companies does not necessarily imply that they inflict a net loss on India. They could easily balance or off-set the outgo in foreign currency on account of imports, repatriated earnings and other remittances by exporting and thus earning equivalent amounts of foreign currency. The TNCs, in particular, command access to superior distribution and marketing systems well suited for channelling exports from India.

Balance of Payments

In keeping with this proposition, the government of India has often stated that foreign financial and technical collaboration agreements are important instruments for promoting exports.

Consequently, the next question to be addressed is whether TNC-affiliated companies in general have shown a better export performance than Indian companies. In continuation of the answer to that question, we will investigate the combined balance-of-payment effects of foreign controlled companies.

In the study by Subramanian and Pillai mentioned above, it was revealed that Indian engineering firms with relatively low degrees of foreign association had a better export performance than firms with higher degrees of foreign association.[29] The same pattern emerged with respect to dyestuffs and intermediates.[30] As for drugs and pharmaceuticals, no significant correlation between the degree of foreign association and export performance could be identified.[31] This implies that foreign-affiliated companies did not perform better than Indian controlled companies with regard to exports.

The same general conclusion may be drawn from the figures presented in Table 4.12. They show that 276 foreign controlled companies in the mid-1970s earned foreign exchange equal to between 6.1 and 7.4 per cent of net sales. During the same period, earnings of 1077 Indian companies varied between 6.1 and 7.3 per cent of net sales. In other words, foreign controlled companies did not apply their superior global distribution and marketing systems in order to enhance exports from India.

This situation has not changed significantly since 1978. Some of the larger TNC subsidiaries have indeed increased exports as compared to total net sales, partly with a view to obtaining preferential treatment under FERA. But considered as a group, foreign controlled companies do not seem to export relatively more than Indian controlled firms.[32]

Table 4.12

Earnings in Foreign Exchange to Net Sales for Indian and Foreign Controlled Companies, 1975-76 to 1977-78

Percentages

	1975-76	1976-77	1977-78
Indian companies (1077)	6.1	7.3	6.9
Foreign controlled Rupee companies (276)	6.1	7.4	7.0

Source: RBI, 'Foreign Exchange Earnings and Outgo by Medium and Large Processing and Manufacturing Companies, 1975-76 to 1977-78', *Reserve Bank of India Bulletin*, July 1981, Statement 2, p 580.

Furthermore, recently published data show a decline in the export performance of foreign controlled companies. RBI studies display a falling ratio of exports to net sales.[33] A comprehensive study undertaken by the Corporate Studies Group at the Indian Institute of Public Administration reveals the same general pattern.[34]

It is evident from the above that neither FERA nor the government's export promotion policies have brought about the effects intended.[35] To make things worse, the whole private corporate sector's earnings in foreign currency as a percentage of net sales has also declined since 1976-77, as can be inferred from Table 4.17 below. Most likely, this decline reflects the overall recessionary conditions in India's export markets, especially the OECD countries and OPEC. Still, it remains to be explained why foreign controlled companies operating in India have not done more to neutralize the effects of the global recession, assuming, of course, that it would be in their power to do so.

The matter was raised during discussions with TNC representatives in 1979 and 1983. It is interesting to note that most of the managers interviewed explained the relatively low export performance by referring to the fact that they had come to India, not in order to produce for exports, but to take advantage of the growing domestic market. A few notable exceptions were found, however, amongst British controlled companies engaged in tea, tobacco and other 'traditional' sectors.

It is a matter of concern that the Indian government has failed to enforce its export promotion and foreign exchange conservation policies.

Leaving aside the distortion of effects, which may to some extent be explained by forces beyond the government's control, it remains particularly surprising that the imposition of export restrictions in connection with foreign collaboration agreements was allowed to continue after the mid-1970s. According to the RBI, the use of these restrictive business practices were even permitted to increase during the late 1970s.[36] According to unofficial sources, the frequency with which export restriction clauses have been imposed has gone up further since 1981.[37]

It should be noted, furthermore, that certain aspects of the export promotion policies have worked against attaining the objectives embodied in FERA and the industrial approval system. This is so, in particular, with respect to the concessions given to 'Export Houses and Trading Houses'.[38] Several TNC-affiliated companies have managed to get themselves registered under these schemes, thus securing for themselves exceptional treatment. The manner in which they have obtained status as 'Export Houses' or 'Trading Houses' is often such that it can only be characterised as exploitation of loopholes in the regulatory framework. This is the case, for instance, when a company manufacturing electronics starts exporting marine products in order to obtain the benefits and exemptions enjoyed by 'Export Houses'.[39]

The major point here, however, is that the export promotion policies pursued by the Indian government are not all properly coordinated with the policy framework aimed at extracting the maximum net benefits from TNC operations. Permitting a TNC subsidiary in the electronics sector to increase imports and expand production on account of increased marine products export is not in keeping with this policy framework, especially not since a large part of the earnings are in rupees while the imports are paid for in 'hard' currencies.[40]

High import content and low export performance of foreign controlled companies have combined to bring about negative balance-of-payments effects. This was shown in the aforementioned study by Subramanian and Pillai with respect to the engineering goods industry and the chemical industry. In another study, by S.K.Goyal, it was revealed that the direct balance-of-payments effects of 189 foreign controlled companies were negative during the year of reference, i.e., 1975-76. The net foreign exchange drain imposed by these companies amounted to Rs. 856 million — or if we exclude oil imports — Rs. 139 million.[41]

Data related to the late 1970s and early 1980s display a similar pattern. The official corporate statistics of the RBI thus show that the direct balance-of-payments effect of 313 foreign controlled companies remained negative over the period from 1975-76 to 1980-81. The figures are presented here in Table 4.13.

A more recent study, undertaken by the Corporate Studies Group and the present author, is summed up in Table 4.14. It further substantiates the general conclusion that foreign controlled companies in India inflict upon that country a quite considerable drain of foreign exchange. In 1983-84 this drain amounted to the equivalent of Rs. 190 crores.

The significance of these figures becomes even more clear when a comparison is made between foreign controlled and Indian dominated firms. The most comprehensive comparative study so far was published by the RBI in 1981.[42] It covered 1353 medium and large companies in the processing and manufacturing industry groups. The study included 276 foreign controlled companies. The most pertinent results of the study have been summed up in Table 4.15.

Comparing Indian and foreign controlled companies it is worthy of note that, over the three-year period studied by the RBI, the earnings in foreign exchange of the latter were completely off-set by the outgo in foreign currency. The combined direct effect on the balance of payments was negative — to the tune of Rs. 2 crores. On the other hand, the Indian companies provided a surplus of more than Rs. 365 crores.

Table 4.13

Earnings and Expenditure in Foreign Exchange of 313 Foreign Controlled Rupee Companies, 1975-76, 1979-80 and 1980-81

Rs. lakhs

	1975-76	1979-80	1980-81
Earnings in foreign exchange	215,61	325,31	368,60
Of which:			
- Exports	206,21	303,34	355,56
Expenditure in foreign exchange	234,34	461,64	530,58
Of which:			
- Imports	193,21	390,59	458,22
Direct balance-of -payment effect	(-)18,73	(-)136,33	(-)161,98

Source: As for Table 4.3, Statements 16, 17 and 18, pp 342-346.

Table 4.16 presents data on earnings and expenditure according to the country of controlling interest. It should be noted here that British controlled firms as a group had a considerable positive net impact on the balance of payments during the first three-year period, whereas US controlled companies had an overall negative net impact. This difference to some extent reflected the dissimilar sectoral compositions of British and American investments in India. But as American and West German investments were basically alike in that respect, and as the latter had a positive net impact, differences with regard to corporate strategy cannot be ruled out.[42]

Table 4.14
Foreign Exchange Utilisation and Earnings by 190 Foreign Controlled Companies, 1980-81 and 1983-84

Rs. lakhs

	1980-81		1983-84	
	36 subsidiaries	154 FCCs	36 subsidiaries	154 FCCs
Imports	124,36	365,22	130,17	483,23
Other expenditure in foreign currency	7,25	24,42	8,01	29,82
Of which – Royalty	57	3,55	41	3,86
– Interest	23	1,98	2,38	4,73
Dividends remitted	14,63	33,59	17,76	49,39
Total outgo in foreign currency	146,24	423,23	155,94	562,44
Total earnings in foreign currency	114,85	287,48	153,51	371,87
Direct balance-of-payments effect	(-) 31,39	(-)135,75	(-) 2,43	(-)190,57

Note: The companies included in the Table are those with more than 25 per cent foreign equity covered in a sample of 405 large companies. This sample includes almost all registered companies with more than Rs 1 crore risk capital which, at the same time, have been in operation for at least ten years before 1984. The abbreviation 'FCC' stands for 'Foreign Controlled Companies' other than 'subsidiaries', i.e., the companies with foreign equity ranging from 25 per cent to 50 per cent.

Source: Company annual reports in the Corporate Studies Information System, Indian Institute of Public Administration, New Delhi.

Table 4.15

Earnings and Expenditure in Foreign Exchange of Indian and Foreign Controlled Companies

Rs. lakhs

	1975-76	1976-77	1977-78
Earnings in foreign exchange	680,13	916,95	936,43
Expenditure in foreign exchange	577,22	652,97	939,75
Direct Balance-of-Payments effect	+102,91	+263,98	(−) 3,32
Indian companies (1077)			
Earnings	471,33	631,52	651,79
Expenditure	349,56	388,34	651,28
Direct B-of-P effect	+121,77	+243,28	+ 51
Foreign controlled companies (276)			
Earnings	208,80	285,43	284,64
Expenditure	227,66	264,73	288,47
Direct B-of-P effect	(−) 18,86	+ 20,70	(−) 3,83

Source: RBI, 'Foreign Exchange Earnings and Outgo by Medium and Large Processing and Manufacturing Companies, 1975-76 to 1977-78', *RBI Bulletin*, July 1981.

Such differences in corporate strategy were somewhat blurred during the second period considered in Table 4.15. While the data referring to 1979-80 and 1980-81 are not directly comparable to those referring to the earlier period, it remains significant that they reveal negative balance-of-payments effects

Table 4.16

Earnings and Expenditure in Foreign Exchange of FCRCs According to the Country of Controlling Interest 1975–76 to 1977–78 and 1979–80 to 1980–81

Rs. lakhs

	Earnings in foreign exchange	Expenditure	Direct B-of-P effect (+/-)	Total for 2-year and 3-year period
UK (134)				
1975-76	129,88	113,15	+16,73	
1976-77	162,59	121,25	+41,34	+82,75
1977-78	166,73	142,05	+24,68	
(150)				
1979-80	195,27	192,83	+ 2,44	
1980-81	227,99	250,11	-22,12	-19,68
USA (61)				
1975-76	16,39	40,85	-24,46	
1976-77	32,46	52,26	-19,80	-64,53
1977-78	32,75	53,02	-20,27	
(72)				
1979-80	30,74	129,04	-98,30	
1980-81	34,00	120,78	-86,78	-185,08
West Germany (24)				
1975-76	29,09	25,76	+ 3,33	
1976-77	26,30	24,09	+ 2,21	+8,70
1977-78	31,87	28,71	+ 3,16	
(33)				
1979-80	39,52	52,32	-12,80	
1980-81	45,09	64,76	-19,67	-32,47
Switzerland (14)				
1975-76	14,56	15,66	- 1,10	
1976-77	26,34	16,51	+ 9,83	+14,48
1977-78	28,66	22,91	+ 5,75	
(16)				
1979-80	17,79	32,86	-15,07	
1980-81	20,86	34,51	-13,65	-28,72
Other countries (43)				
1975-76	18,87	32,25	-13,38	
1976-77	37,75	50,63	-12,88	-43,41
1977-78	24,63	41,78	-17,15	
(42)				
1979-80	41,99	54,61	-12,62	
1980-81	40,65	60,42	-19,77	-32,39

Sources: 1975-76 to 1977-78: As for Table 4.10, Statement 2, pp 581-583.
1979-80 and 1980-81: As for Table 4.3, Statements 16, 17 and 18, pp 342-346.

Table 4.17 Earnings and Expenditure in Foreign Currency by the Corporate Sector, 1975-76 to 1982-83

	1975-76	1976-77	1977-78	1978-79	1979-80	1980-81	1981-82	1982-82
Total earnings in foreign currency	849,40	1157,68	1224,09	1105,89	1219,56	1363,28	1665,69	1776,11
- of which								
Engineering	210,03	276,01	311,67	316,65	318,75	367,24	461,28	505,98
Chemicals	71,46	92,09	97,92	116,20	141,64	168,43	253,55	257,62
Group III industries	284,85	348,16	345,83	269,89	355,29	366,17	211,99	226,97
Total expenditure in foreign currency	601,31	681,40	978,64	1110,30	1373,81	1560,62	2109,61	2287,35
- of which								
Engineering	265,08	279,66	288,07	344,20	504,53	614,48	368,47	885,91
Chemicals	127,66	149,20	211,47	222,50	280,15	329,61	340,77	523,51
Group III industries	70,41	92,37	243,61	244,28	209,81	197,78	208,03	245,31
Direct Balance of Payments effects	248,09	476,28	245,45	-4,41	-154,25	-197,34	-443,92	-511,24
- of which								
Engineering	-55,05	-3,65	23,60	-27,55	-185,78	-247,24	-407,19	-379,93
Chemicals	-56,20	-57,11	-113,55	-106,30	-138,51	-161,18	-197,22	-265,89
Group III Industries	214,44	255,79	102,22	25,61	145,48	168,39	3,96	-18,34
Percentages:								
Earnings to net sales	6.5	7.9	7.7	6.3	6.0	5.7	5.7	5.6

Note: Group III-industries include edible oils, sugar, other food products, tobacco, cotton textiles, jute textiles, silk and rayon textiles, woolen textiles, breweries and distilleries. Only some of these industries could be included in the figures for 1981-82 and 1982-83 due to changes in the RBI statements.
Sources: As for Table 4.2.

with respect to all the four countries mentioned as well as to the group of 'other countries'. This was a disturbing change - and not at all in keeping with government policies and intentions.

Table 4.17 presents aggregate data for the corporate sector as a whole in addition to information about the foreign currency earnings and expenditure of three major industry groups. The pattern which emerges from this Table indicates that chemical industries as a group had a negative net impact on the balance of payments every year during the eight-year period investigated. Consumer goods industries, on the other hand, had a positive net impact until 1982. Engineering had a positive net impact in just one year, 1977-78. Since then, the engineering sector has imposed an increasing foreign exchange burden on India.

The total impact of the private corporate sector was positive during the first three-year period, but turned negative - and increasingly so - during the second three-year period. This trend continued in 1981-82 and 1982-83.

Parallel to this development, earnings in foreign currency as a percentage of net sales continued to decline from a peak in 1976-77, when it stood at 7.9 per cent, to 5.6 per cent in 1982-83. This trend reflected the increasing relative importance of the domestic market as opposed to the export markets abroad.

These patterns and trends, described in the preceding paragraphs, were basically in contradiction with the official policy of import substitution and export expansion. Paradoxically, FERA and the industrial licensing policies may have contributed to the unintended evolution, in the sense that these policies have acted as pressures on foreign companies to bring down their engagements in consumer goods and other 'light' industries, where they had extensive export potentials. Instead, they were impelled to expand their operations in engineering and chemicals, where they had neither an interest in nor the same potentials for export. At the same time, this shift to more technology-intensive sectors prompted a substantial increase in imports and technical payments. These and other aspects, it appears, were not properly considered and taken into account when the various instruments of policy were evolved in the mid-1970s and later.

Notes and References

1. Cf. Chapter 2, note 21.
2. This was reiterated in the Industrial Policy Statement of 1977 which read: 'For all approved foreign investments, there will be complete freedom for remittance of profits, royalties, dividends as well as repatriation of capital subject, of course, to rules and regulations common to all.' Government of India, *Guidelines for Industries*, (1979), *op.cit.*, Part I, Sec. II, p 14.
3. S.K.Goyal emphasized these basic assumptions in *Some Aspects of the Operations of Multinational Corporations in India*, New Delhi, Indian Institute of Public Administration, n.d. (1981), p 8 ff. High-ranking government officials, during discussions in 1983, admitted that the assumptions mentioned were indeed essential elements in the considerations that led to the formulation of the FERA provisions. But some of them added that government became aware quite soon of the very limited validity of the second and third assumptions.
4. Cf. the study mentioned as source for Table 4.1.
5. It was an amendment to the Companies Act in 1973 that made it obligatory for joint stock companies to furnish information on remittances abroad on account of dividends.
6. This impression is based on various samples of companies and on aggregate information on remittances.

It is known from these latter sources that the amount of dividends paid abroad was exceptionally small during 1974-75, and comparatively small during the following year. See, e.g., S.L.Kapur, *op.cit.*, Annex V, p 47.

7. RBI, 'Finances of Foreign Controlled Rupee Companies, 1975-76 to 1980-81', *Reserve Bank of India Bulletin*, August 1984.

8. Cf. Government of India, *Guidelines for Industries 1976-77*, *op.cit.*, Appendix XVI, pp 131-138. Several new items were added to the list in 1978; cf. *Guidelines for Industries* (1982), *op.cit.*, Sec. I, pp 18-19. This revised policy, however, came into effect so late during the period studied here that it has been disregarded in the grouping of industries in Table 4.

9. Data on all the 1720 companies included in the RBI studies have been processed in the same way as those included in Table 4.4.

10. Cf. p 15 f. above.

11. Optimistic evaluations of future business prospects in India can be found in most annual reports of TNC-affiliated companies in the country. Similar, although somewhat more cautious statements have been published by business magazines and dailies on numerous occasions over the last decade. This does not imply, though, that TNCs in general have expressed satisfaction with the conditions prevailing in India, including the politically determined conditions. With respect to these latter conditions American and British firms, especially, have actually expressed strong dissatisfaction several times, mainly during the period 1977-80.

12. This statement is based on extensive comparisons of changes in assets of foreign controlled subsidiaries with those of selected Indian companies.

13. Detailed information relating to the top 20 TNC subsidiaries is presented in S.K.Goyal, *Some Aspects of the Operations of Multinational Corporations in India*, *op.cit.*, p 11 ff.

14. This concept refers to the difference between receipts and money outlays incurred directly in carrying on the operations of the company.

15. Cf. Chapter 1 above.

16. RBI, 'Foreign Exchange Earnings and Outgo by Medium and Large Processing and Manufacturing Companies, 1975-76 to 1977-78', *Reserve Bank of India Bulletin*, July 1981, Statement 2, p 580.

17. A similar pattern of foreign exchange utilization emerged from a study carried out by S.K.Goyal on the basis of company balance sheets relating to the year 1975-76. See S.K.Goyal, *The Impact of Foreign Subsidiaries on India's Balance of Payments*, New Delhi, Indian Institute of Public Administration, 1979, Table XI, p 59.

18. S.K.Goyal has reached the same general conclusion in various studies; see, e.g., Goyal, *Some Aspects of the Operations of Multinational Companies in India*, op.cit., p 15.

19. Cf. the first section of this Chapter.

20. This was pointed out also in: Neela Mukherjee, 'Technical Payments Abroad', *Economic Times*, November 16, 1983.

21. A study undertaken by RBI showed that, during the six-year period 1964-70, technical payments for the private sector as a whole came to 46 per cent of dividends for all firms, whereas it came to 23 per cent for foreign majority-owned firms and 75 (sic!) per cent for foreign minority-owned companies. See RBI, 'Survey of Foreign Financial and Technical Collaboration in Indian Industry 1964-70', *Reserve Bank of India Bulletin*, June 1974. In a study of 45 companies, Lall and Streeten found that technical payments amounted to 32 per cent for the sample as a whole, including Indian firms. The equivalent figures for foreign majority-owned companies and foreign minority-owned amounted to 16 and 135 (sic!) per cent, respectively, Cf. Lall & Streeten, op.cit., p 146.

22. Cf. Appendix V below.

23. In 1982-83, a year not included in the Appendix table, imports to the chemical industries continued to account for almost 90 per cent of total foreign exchange utilization. Cf. RBI, 'Finances of Medium and Large Public Limited Companies, 1982-83', op.cit., Table 10, p 119 ff.

24. See the first section of this Chapter.

25. RBI has not yet published data directly comparable to those shown in Table 4.10. But on the basis of the 1980-81 survey of medium and large companies, the ratio may be calculated for the 1720 companies included. It turns out to be 12.3 per cent for 1978-79; 12.5 per cent for 1979-80; and 13.8 per cent for 1980-81. Cf. *Reserve Bank of India Bulletin*, July 1983, Table 3, p 294 ff.

Balance of Payments 133

26. Subramanian and Pillai, *Multinationals and Indian Export*, New Delhi, Allied Publishers, 1979, p 28 ff.
27. *Ibid.*, pp 43 f; 53 f.
28. RBI, *Foreign Collaboration in Indian Industry Fourth Survey*, *op.cit.*, p 29 ff.
29. Subramanian and Pillai, *op.cit.*, p 25 ff.
30. *Ibid.*, p 53 f.
31. *Ibid.*, p 43 f.
32. This conclusion is supported in a recent study by Nagesh Kumar. On the basis of primary financial statistics of 1334 medium and large public limited manufacturing companies - with reference to the year 1980-81 - Kumar has worked out the proportion of exports in total sales for foreign and Indian controlled enterprises, respectively. Foreign controlled enterprises are defined as those with at least 25 per cent foreign equity. His analysis reveals only a marginally higher propensity to export on the part of foreign controlled companies - 0.051 compared to 0.049 for Indian controlled companies. There is no common tendency across the 43 industries considered. In 21 of these, the foreign controlled firms have higher export ratios, but this is not the case in the remaining 22 industries, where Indian controlled companies have the higher ratios. The general conclusion to be drawn from Kumar's analysis is that the export performance of TNC-affiliated companies in India do not appear to be significantly different from that of their local counterparts. Cf. Nagesh Kumar, *Multinational Enterprises and Export Promotion: The Case of India*, New Delhi, Research and Information System for Non-Aligned and Other Developing Countries, 1987.
33. The exports-sales ratio for foreign controlled companies in the RBI sample was down to 5.9 per cent in 1979-80, and 5.7 per cent in 1980-81. The ratios may be calculated on the basis of data in Table 4.17 below and in the *Reserve Bank of India Bulletin*, August 1984, Statement 3, p 307. Cf. also A.K. Bagchi, 'Foreign Collaboration in Indian Industry', *EPW*, May 24, 1986, Table 1, p 915.
34. According to this study, the exports-sales ratio for 181 large companies with more than 10 per cent foreign equity fell from 7.0 in the three-year period 1975-1978 to 5.5 in 1981-1984. Cf. K.S.Chalapati

Rao, *India's Export Policies and Performance: An Evaluation*, New Delhi, Indian Institute of Public Administration, 1987, Table XIV, p 87.

35. Cf. Chapter 2 above.
36. Observed in: RBI, *Foreign Collaboration in Indian Industry. Fourth Survey*, op.cit., p 41.
37. This was revealed by participants at the seminar, 'The Impact of Multinational Corporations on India's Position in the International Division of Labour', New Delhi, January 1988.
38. Cf. K.S.Chalapati Rao, op.cit., p 27 f.
39. This and several other examples are described in detail, *ibid.*, p 91 ff.
40. The USSR and the Eastern European countries, with which India's trade is conducted in rupees, have become the main export markets for a very large number of TNC-affiliated companies. See, *ibid.*, for further information.
41. S.K.Goyal, *The Impact of Foreign Subsidiaries on India's Balance of Payments*, op.cit.
42. RBI, 'Foreign Exchange Earnings and Outgo by Medium and Large Processing and Manufacturing Companies, 1975-78', *RBI Bulletin*, July 1981.
43. Actually, it was my clear impression from discussions with TNC managers that the American controlled subsidiaries were more inclined than others to extract the maximum surplus from their operations in India, partly because they were pessimistic about future business prospects in the country. There were, however, indications of change in 1983 as compared to 1979, in the sense that even American subsidiaries expected to expand their operations appreciably.

• CHAPTER 5 •

Effects of the Regulations on Transfer of Resources

Foreign investment and technology may provide positive contributions to the host economy. The aim of regulation and control is therefore not simply to curtail the activities of foreign firms in the host country, but rather to shape these activities in accordance with national objectives and priorities.

This has been, for many years, the basic thinking behind Indian policies governing foreign investment and transfer of technology. More specifically, the regulatory framework enacted in 1974 aimed at controlling foreign exchange transactions with a further view to conserving foreign exchange resources. By implication, the regulations were intended not to affect the inflow of capital and technology. If anything, they should stimulate these inflows. Besides, the regulations were framed in such a manner that foreign companies were either forced to, or acquired an interest in, channelling their investible resources and technology according to priorities fixed in Indian development plans.

In the preceding Chapter we studied the effects of the regulations on dividend remittances, expenditure in foreign currency and the foreign companies' net impact on India's balance of payments. In this Chapter we shall focus on possible influences on the flows of foreign capital and technology. Sectoral allocations and diversification of activities will be considered in the next Chapter.

Effects on Provision of Capital

The implementation of the FERA provisions with regard to foreign equity participation directly affected the net inflow of foreign capital. Certainly, most of the foreign controlled companies instructed to dilute chose to do so by raising new capital from the Indian capital market. Consequently, their actions did not directly affect the net inflow of foreign capital. But other companies chose to disinvest foreign holdings in order to reduce non-resident participation, thus transferring capital abroad.

Table 5.1 summarises data on the dilution of foreign equity holdings in the crucial per-

Table 5.1

Dilution of Foreign Equity Holdings by FERA Companies, 1976-1980

Amounts in Rs. mill.

	Fresh issues to Indians		Fresh issues to Foreigners		Disinvestment of foreign holdings	
	Number	Amount	Number	Amount	Number	Amount
1976	17	146.0	3	3.3	1	4.0
1977	25	185.2	-	-	6	43.9
1978	36	243.0	18	187.5	15	132.6
1979	22	97.7	7	51.7	11	124.7
1980	3	14.6	2	10.2	2	6.1

Source: RBI, 'Trends in Consents for Issue of Capital and Public Response to Capital Issues During 1976-1980', *Reserve Bank of India Bulletin*, February 1982, Table 6, p 85.

iod from 1976 to 1980. As can be seen from the Table, 35 consents were given by the Controller of Capital Issues for disinvestment of a total amount of Rs. 311 million. During the same period, fresh issues to non-residents came to no more than Rs. 253 million. As a result, the dilution of foreign equity holdings by FERA companies over the five-year period implied an outgo of capital to the tune of Rs. 58 million.[1]

Critics of the new policy had warned government that restrictions on foreign ownership would not only result in disinvestments but also deter foreign corporations from investing in India.

Indian industrialists interviewed in 1977 expressed some concern, but only a small minority was in favour of relaxing the restrictions. The strongest criticism came from abroad, especially from American businessmen. Orville Freeman, then President of Business International and co-Chairman of the Indo-US Business Council, advanced his criticism in this manner in 1977: 'The biggest constraint now is you cannot have more than 40 per cent ownership except in core industries, or for export. India should no longer discriminate against outside investment. I am not presuming to tell the Indian Government what to do, but restrictions on investment by limiting ownership are clearly a deterrent. And if India chooses to have these restrictions it is going to have an adverse effect. This is purely a statement of fact.'[2]

The contention implied in this statement is very difficult to test. Even provided a decline in foreign investments received by India could be ascertained, this would not necessarily be an effect of government policies. It is more probable, in fact, that other factors - like the general economic and political 'climate' -

138 *Transnational Corporations in India*

would account for the major part of any decline.[3] In this connection, it should be noted that direct investment flows to the developing countries as a group have contracted sharply since their peak in 1981.[4]

Still, it is worthy of note that the flow of foreign direct investment to India declined drastically in the three-year period after 1975, as shown in Figure 6. During 1977,

Figure 6

Net Inflow of Foreign Direct Investment 1970-1983

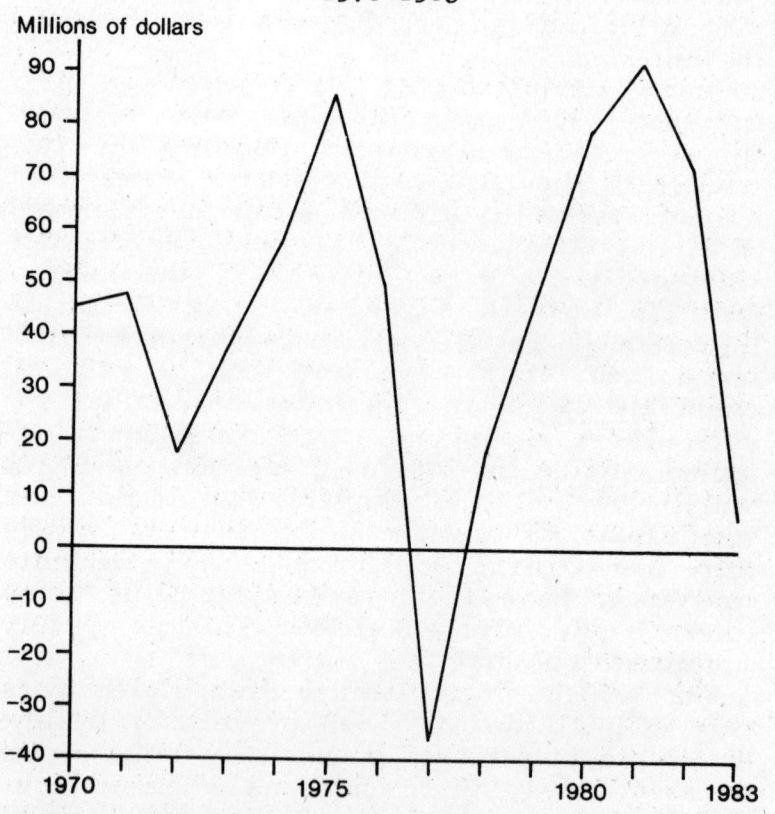

Millions of dollars

Source: UNCTC, *Transnational Corporations in World Development*, Third Survey, op.cit., Annex Table II.13, p 308; and UNCTC, *Trends and Issues in Foreign Direct Investment and Related Flows*, New York, 1985, Table A.4, p 94.

the inflow was even reversed as US$ 36 million were transferred from India to developed market economies. This decline and reversed flow cannot be attributed to any similarly drastic deterioration in business opportunities. Neither the index of industrial production, summarized here in Table 5.2, nor more direct indicators for business prospects, warrant a conclusion to that effect. Thus, it should be noted that foreign controlled companies maintained significantly higher profitability ratios than Indian controlled firms. Besides, there was no trend towards decreasing profitability among foreign controlled companies, as can be inferred from Table 5.3. It may be added that the compound growth rate over the period for operating profits was 10.2 per cent and that for profits after tax amounted to 13.9 per cent.

On this basis, we are tempted to conclude that the enforcement of FERA and the associated industrial regulations did indeed affect the flow of direct investment to India in a negative way, primarily because they created among potential foreign investors an image of India as a somewhat hostile host country.

However, the deterring effects of Indian regulations - assuming their existence - remained short-lived and selective with respect to the impact on capital flows. Already by 1979, direct investment flows from developed countries again reached the same level as before the enforcement of FERA. At the same time, the total stock of direct investment from OECD countries again started increasing after three years of stagnation.[5]

The sharp decline in inflows of foreign direct investment after 1981 cannot be attributed to any new instruments of policy implemented by the Indian government. We propose, instead, an interpretation of this develop-

Table 5.2

Index of Industrial Production, 1974-81
Base: 1980 = 100

	General index	Chemicals	Electrical machinery	Other machinery
1974	113.2	123.0	113.1	152.9
1975	119.2	132.8	120.3	159.6
1976	133.7	155.4	129.9	165.0
1977	138.3	171.6	145.5	179.8
1978	147.7	182.6	151.2	202.2
1979	149.5	187.3	163.3	204.9
1980	150.6	183.3	170.0	220.1
1981	164.6	207.6	180.0	234.1

Source: Government of India, *Economic Survey 1982-83*, Delhi, 1983, Table 1.14, p 94 f.

Table 5.3

Profitability Ratios for Foreign Controlled Companies, 1975-76 to 1980-81

	Gross profits as percentage of sales	Profits after tax as percentage of net worth
1975-76	11.7	12.8
1976-77	12.3	14.0
1977-78	11.5	11.6
1978-79	12.1	13.9
1979-80	12.0	15.2
1980-81	10.9	15.4

Note: The data refer to 313 companies.

Source: RBI, 'Finances of Foreign Controlled Rupee Companies and Branches of Foreign Companies, 1975-76 to 1980-81', *Reserve Bank of India Bulletin*, August 1984, Statement 1, p 301.

ment as a reflection of the general tendency on the part of TNCs to change their mode of involvement from direct investment in wholly owned or majority owned subsidiaries to other forms of involvement.[6]

It is, therefore, of interest to take a closer look at such other forms of involvement.

If we look specifically at foreign equity investment involved in collaboration agreements, a pattern different from the one above emerges. The total number of collaboration agreements, as depicted in Figure 7, stagnated during the period 1975-1979. Over the same period, foreign equity investment involved in those 15-20 per cent of the agreements that included financial participation fluctuated around an only slowly rising trend. But after

Figure 7

Number of Foreign Collaborations Approved and Foreign Equity Investment Involved, 1969-1985

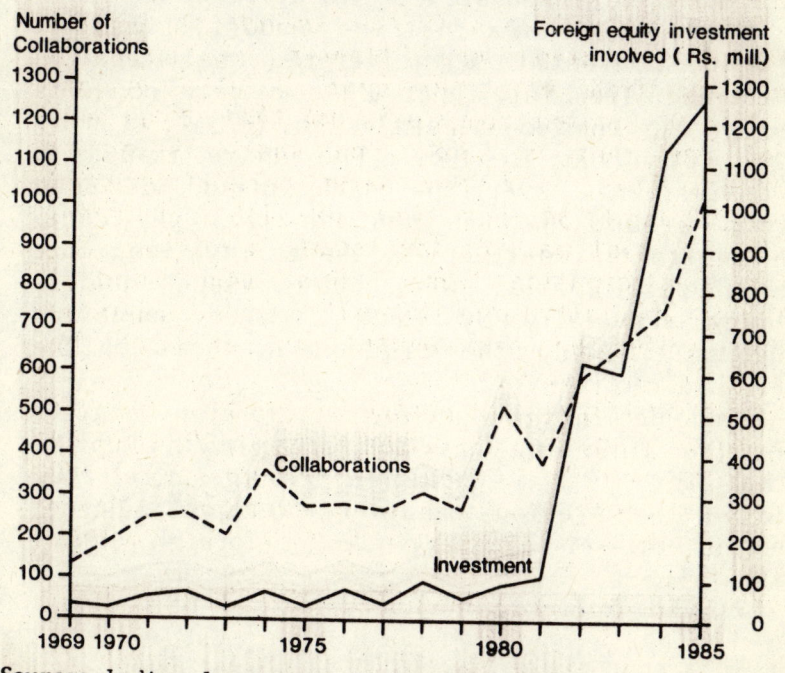

Source: Indian Investment Centre, New Delhi.

1979, and particularly after 1981, both the number of collaborations and the amount of foreign equity investment involved increased appreciably.

More important, perhaps, than these indications of renewed foreign interest in investing in India,[7] were the changes in the pattern of foreign involvement in the corporate sector.

Though not one of the stated primary objectives of FERA, the ownership provisions of the Act clearly aimed for a reduction of foreign financial participation in non-core and non-exporting industries. This would not necessarily result in an overall decline in foreign financial involvement in the corporate sector, as the decline in non-core and non-exporting industries could easily be offset by a corresponding increase of foreign investment in core sectors and export industries. Available data, however, indicate that FERA contributed to bringing down rather drastically foreign participation in corporate capital formation.

Table 5.4 shows that the amount of capital issues[8] consented with foreign participation declined from 61.5 per cent of all consents to public limited companies in 1976 to a mere 29.5 per cent in 1980. The share issued to non-residents over the same period declined from around 34 per cent to 11.3 per cent. A substantial part of the issues involving foreign participation were bonus issues undertaken especially by TNC-affiliated companies before effecting the dilution in terms of the FERA directives.[9]

This declining importance of foreign sources in the financing of corporate growth implied that the foreign exchange leakages, referred to in the previous Chapter, were to a lesser extent off-set by provision of foreign equity capital.

Viewed in a broader perspective, FERA most

Table 5.4

Foreign Participation in Respect of Capital Issues Approved, 1976-80

(Amount in Rs. Mill.)

	Total consents (non-govt. public limited companies)	Of which consents involving foreign participation	Share of non-residents
1976			
Number of consents	279	127	
Amount consented	3,319	2,042	1,126
Percentage to total consents		61.5	33.9
1977			
Number of consents	287	134	
Amount consented	3,474	2,013	1,199
Percentage to total consents		57.9	34.5
1978			
Number of consents	279	126	
Amount consented	2,289	1,277	579
Percentage to total consents		55.8	25.3
1979			
Number of consents	331	117	
Amount consented	4,760	2,230	1,321
Percentage to total consents		46.8	27.8
1980			
Number of consents	358	123	
Amount consented	7,704	2,274	869
Percentage to total consents		29.5	11.3

Source: RBI, 'Trends in Consents for Issue of Capital..', *op.cit.*, Table 5, p 84.

likely accentuated the general tendency toward reducing the importance of foreign direct investment in India.[10] Instead, the new provisions regarding ownership promoted other forms of collaboration with no or only minority financial participation. In addition to the above indications, it is worth noting that foreign participation in respect of *initial* capital issues approved showed a marked decline in the early 1980s.[11]

Not all TNCs, however, reacted in the same manner. With regard to their willingness to provide capital as well as their overall investment and collaboration strategy, they responded quite differently to the changed regulatory framework. Variations in corporate strategies which, in turn, related to production profiles, organisational structures, etc., probably accounted for most of the differences in TNC responses. It is interesting, though, that contours of a pattern emerged also with respect to TNC home countries. Especially the reactions of American TNCs differed from those of most other corporations.

American controlled firms figured prominently in the list of companies that opted to wind up their operations in India instead of diluting their non-resident interest.[12] They also figured conspicuously often in the lists of companies which opposed dilution of non-resident interest to less than 51 per cent. Correspondingly, during interviews, executives of American controlled companies generally expressed much stronger opposition to the new equity rules contained in FERA than did other executives. A more comprehensive study carried out in the early 1980s revealed that American executives were still rather conservative in their approach to India.[13]

As a result of this prevailing attitude, several American corporations have exploited a minimum of business opportunities in the country. The United States is only the second largest investor in India (after the United Kingdom) with less than 19 per cent of total foreign direct investment (1981).[14]

There are indications, however, that American corporate strategies have changed recently. Since 1984, more than 60 new companies have been incorporated in India with American equity capital. The overwhelming majority of these have been set up with 40 per cent or less foreign equity holdings.[15]

The increased interest in collaborating with India on new terms is also reflected in Figure 8. Since 1981, the foreign equity investment involved in technical collaboration agreements has grown significantly, from a level of around Rs. 20 million to around Rs. 300 million, with a peak, in 1985, of almost Rs. 400 million.

The Figure reveals a similar rising trend for the EEC countries as a group. As for Japan, this country's foreign investors showed much greater interest in India from the late 1970s onwards, but the equity investment involved fluctuated considerably from one year to another. The number of technical collaboration agreements grew more steadily over the period, as indicated in Table 5.5.

Summing up, it seems warranted to conclude that FERA did affect the provision of foreign capital, directly by impelling some foreign corporations to disinvest, and indirectly by deterring several others from investing in India. But the set-back to the inflow of foreign capital was only transitory. And by the early 1980s, India attracted more foreign investments than before the enactment of FERA. The importance of foreign *direct* investment, however, continued to decline relative to non-equity forms of collaboration.

Before leaving the subject of capital provi-

Figure 8

Foreign Investment Involved in Collaboration Agreements, 1970–1986

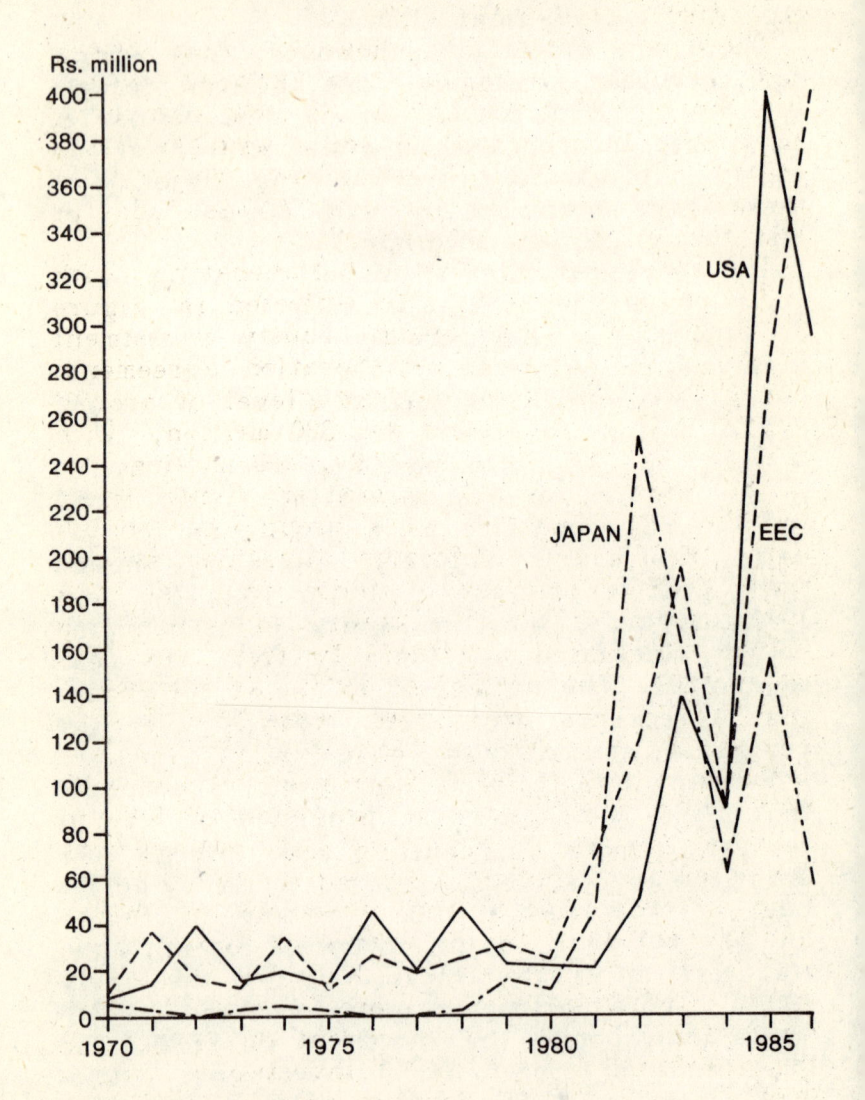

Source: Indian Investment Centre, New Delhi.

sion in this context there is yet another aspect to be taken into consideration, albeit very briefly. That is the effects of the regulations on the behaviour of TNC-affiliated companies in the Indian capital market.

Considering that almost all these companies have continuously expanded their capital base in India, it may be inferred from the above that they have financed this expansion primarily from Indian sources. This was so even before 1974. A study of the 50 largest foreign subsidiaries revealed that foreign sources contributed no more than 5.3 per cent to the growth of these companies during the period from 1956 to 1975.[16] The balance was financed from retained earnings, accumulated depreciation, locally raised loans and equity, and other 'Indian' sources.

Directly comparable data are not available for the period after 1975. But the data presented in Table 5.4 above clearly indicate a declining importance of foreign sources in the financing of the growth of companies with foreign association. A cursory study of some 20 TNC-affiliated companies even indicate a drastic decline in foreign funding.[17] Several of these companies obtained no foreign funds at all during the period from 1974 to 1983.

The question therefore arises whether TNC affiliates have drawn on local savings to such an extent that they have deprived indigenous firms of funds. Available data do not support this contention with respect to the period prior to the enforcement of FERA. But subsequent to the Reserve Bank's issuing of directives for dilution of foreign equity participation, it appears that by enlisting local capital, FERA companies pre-empted scarce capital resources and crowded out potential Indian borrowers. Capital issues by FERA companies were particularly sizable during 1977.

1978 and 1979, accounting for 19 per cent, 14 per cent and 13 per cent, respectively, of all capital issues, including government company issues.[18] The public response to these capital issues was overwhelming: all issues were over-subscribed.[19] During the same period, it was very difficult for Indian companies to obtain equity finance for funding of new industrial ventures.[20] Even after 1979, TNC-affiliated companies maintained their privileged position in the Indian capital market, benefitting from over-subscription to all their capital issues and significant appreciations over paid-up value.[21] Conversely, new issues and further issues from companies other than those belonging to the large, established Indian business houses were generally under-subscribed between 1979 and 1983.[22]

It should be added, however, that the extensive selling of stock in India by well-known, financially secure and profitable TNC affiliates simultaneously contributed to developing the country's capital market institutions. Since the mid-1970s, Indian capital markets have expanded considerably, providing the corporate sector as a whole with future prospects of raising appreciably larger funds for expansion.[23]

Effects on Provision of Technology

The enactment of the FERA provisions regarding foreign equity participation only marginally affected the inflow of foreign technology. No more than 15 per cent of all collaboration agreements approved during the decade after 1969 involved financial participation. The overwhelming majority of the agreements were for supply of technology against either lump-sum or royalty payment. Thus, these agreements were not directly affected by the implementation of FERA.

Nevertheless, it appears that the integration of the controls governing transfer of technology into the overall regulatory framework pertaining to foreign participation in India's economic development did influence the provision of foreign technology, especially during the period 1975-1979. Foreign business representatives, interviewed in 1977 and 1979, complained about the limits to the duration of agreements to five years after the gestation period. They complained, furthermore, about the limits to royalty payments and the high tax rates on royalty. Most important, perhaps, was their annoyance with the time-consuming case-by-case - and in their opinion arbitrary administration of the policy guidelines.

As a result, the number of collaboration agreements submitted for government approval stagnated after 1974.[24] The number of agreements authorised similarly stagnated, as can be inferred from Figure 7 above.

Partly as a reaction to this development, government in 1977 and again in 1980 modified the policy guidelines, shifting the emphasis from the principle of 'indigenous availability' to 'the necessity for continued inflow of sophisticated and high priority areas'.[25] The limits to the duration of the agreements were raised and exemptions to even these new limits were granted on a liberal basis. Restrictions on royalty payments were relaxed and in respect to lumpsum payments the parties, were permitted to agree that the taxes would be borne exclusively by the Indian party. At the same time, the administration of the industrial approval system was streamlined, the processing of applications speeded up, and the share of rejections brought down from almost 30 per cent in 1975 to 15 per cent and below in 1980 and 1981.[26]

As a result of these and other changes in

the policies pursued and in related administrative procedures, foreign firms commanding technology in demand began responding more favourably to Indian inquiries.[27] Some business representatives, interviewed in 1983, still complained about restrictions and limitations on their freedom of action, but most of these belonged to comparatively small foreign enterprises and newcomers to the Indian market. Executives of large TNCs and corporations familiar with India from several years of experience with business collaboration in the country generally agreed that the policies pursued by the early 1980s were much more conducive to technology transfer than those followed previously.[28] Official representatives of European and American capital even published statements to that effect.[29]

The combined effect of the said changes in policies and attitudes of potential technology suppliers revealed itself in the form of a significant increase in the number of concluded foreign collaboration agreements after 1979. During the preceding five-year period, a total of 1389 agreements were concluded and approved by government. During the subsequent five years, the corresponding figure was 2614.[30]

The country-wise break-up of the collaborations approved with major TNC home countries is shown in Table 5.5. The Table reveals fluctuations and patterns for most of the countries similar to those observed with respect to the total number of collaborations. The Table also shows, however, the significantly increased presence of Japanese firms. It is worthy of note that the number of collaboration agreements concluded with Japanese companies rose steadily after 1981, while the foreign investment involved fluctuated considerably (see Figure 8). A closer scrutiny of the individual agreements indicates that the fluctuations may be attributed to a comparatively small number of technical-cum-financial collaborations, while the continuous increase in the number of agreements concluded reflects a predominant preference among Japanese firms for non-financial forms of cooperation.[31]

Table 5.5

Number of Foreign Collaborations Approved, Selected Countries, 1970-1982

Year	USA	UK	FRG	France	Italy	Switzerland	Japan
1970	33	39	36	7	8	13	15
1971	43	55	42	16	4	14	35
1972	62	38	49	14	8	15	27
1973	48	53	60	13	5	10	38
1974	79	59	71	22	16	33	28
1975	55	54	59	13	10	27	23
1976	69	54	58	17	8	22	10
1977	54	59	55	14	10	23	20
1978	59	61	58	21	13	18	28
1979	48	63	55	17	16	14	12
1980	125	110	100	24	25	38	34
1981	85	79	74	23	18	26	27
1982	110	107	110	28	37	41	51
1983	135	119	129	40	30	47	58
1984	147	126	135	36	37	30	78
1985	197	147	180	61	56	42	108
1986	189	130	183	39	58	32	111

Source: Indian Investment Centre, New Delhi.

Product-wise, the greatest number of collaboration agreements has been authorised in respect of industrial machinery followed by electrical equipment and chemicals other than fertilisers.[32] A cross tabulation of country-wise and product-wise break-ups reveals a pattern which may be depicted as in Table 5.6. Only a few selected countries and principal sectors are shown.

A closer look at the collaborations shows that they have been concentrated in sectors that are technology intensive even by international standards.[33] But the technology transferred has not always been up to contempor-

Table 5.6

Sectors of Concentration in India's Foreign Collaboration by Country

	USA	UK	FRG	Japan	Switzerland	France	Italy
Electronics	X	X		X		X	
Industrial machinery	X	X	X	X	X		X
Auto auxilliaries	X			X			X
Chemicals	X		X	X		X	X
Machine tools		X	X		X		
Telecommunications						X	

Source: Partly based on India International Inc., *Doing Business Collaborations in India, op.cit.,* Table I-13, p 41. Italy has been added and a few changes have been introduced on the basis of our own cross tabulations with reference to the period 1970 to 1983.

ary international standards. Actually, while Indian business representatives have generally lauded government policies for their effects with respect to cost reductions, avoidance of undesirable and restrictive provisions, and unpackaging of technology, they have at the same time complained about the effects with regard to the extent of supplementary technological assistance, updating and upgrading. Furthermore, it has proved difficult for both public and private sector undertakings to obtain access to several types of technology. The Indian petrochemical industry and electronics industry, for example, have experienced difficulties procuring supplementary technological assistance and updated technology.[34] In certain instances, the Indian parties have been able to obtain necessary assistance and relevant advanced technology from Eastern European sources,[35] thus rendering superfluous the concerned suppliers among TNCs.[36] But in a number of cases, this option has not been open to India for the simple reason that TNCs have been in full control of the supply of the technologies in question.

The general impression is that a number of Indian firms, public as well as private sector undertakings, have had difficulties obtaining access to updated, advanced technology. And when such technology has actually been procured, the licensees have often not been able to obtain required technical support from the suppliers, especially as regards support for adapting and modifying the technology transferred to Indian conditions. The major problem – according to Indian business representatives – has not been how to modify the overwhelmingly capital-intensive and labour-saving technologies to suit the reverse factor endowment of India. More importance was attached to the fact that most technologies supplied by

TNCs have been designed for use in large-scale plants. Hence they have proved unsuitable in a number of cases where the existing market in India has been small and export potentials limited.

These and related difficulties cannot, however, be attributed primarily to the policies governing transfer of technology. When asked, some foreign business representatives did refer to restrictive and inflexible policies and their unfavourable impact on profitability. But more thorough inquiries revealed that most foreign business representatives conceived of the financial returns as only marginally influenced by government regulation of technology transfer. Approved royalty and lumpsum payments have normally constituted merely a fraction of total financial returns, the major share emanating from the sales of machinery and other goods associated with the collaboration agreements.[37] Consequently, government's import policies were of greater importance. As these policies were subjected to successive 'liberalisations' in the period after 1979, obstacles to obtaining satisfactory financial returns were concomitantly removed.[38]

This did not, however, eliminate the reticence on the part of international technology suppliers. It is, therefore, necessary to look for other explanatory factors. During our investigations we came across at least one such factor, namely that some technology suppliers, especially among TNCs with extensive operations and interests in LDCs, feared that Indian industry might be able to exploit the technologies transferred for increasing export in competition with the licensers.[39] As a corollary, most foreign business representatives strongly opposed the government's insistence on the Indian licensees' written permission to export to all markets other than those where the technology supplier already has licensees or subsidiaries.[40]

Several foreign business representatives mentioned as justification for their fears the conflict between Piaggio of Italy and Bajaj Auto. Until 1971, Bajaj had manufactured Vespa scooters for the Indian market on licence from Piaggio and in close technical collaboration with that corporation. The agreement was terminated in 1971 in an atmosphere of mutual understanding. Bajaj Auto continued manufacturing what was essentially the Italian Vespa scooter, but marketed the two-wheeler under its own brand name. About a decade later, Piaggio filed suits against Bajaj Auto in the United States, Federal Republic of Germany, UK and Hong Kong, claiming that the former Indian licensee had copied unlawfully the Vespa scooter. What prompted the Italian firm to take these steps, however, was not the fact that Bajaj continued manufacturing scooters similar (though less so over the years) to those of Piaggio's, but rather that the Indian firm, by the late 1970s, had successfully entered foreign markets, primarily in Asia, but with increasing sales even in Western Europe and the U.S. By 1980, Bajaj Auto was the World's second largest producer of scooters with total sales amounting to around 25 per cent of Piaggio's. Thus the former Indian licensee had, unexpectedly, become a threat to the Italian corporation which, under these circumstances, had to safeguard its own export interests by curtailing the exports of Bajaj. Piaggio succeeded in this endeavour and even managed to force Bajaj on the defensive in the Indian market through technical collaboration with Lohia Machines, previously an unimportant indigenous competitor in the two-wheeler industry, but after the agreement a potential rival of Bajaj Auto.

Taught by this and less conspicuous experiences with Indian firms' successful exploitation of technical collaborations, several TNCs have abstained from licensing their technology to Indian partners, or they have insisted on clauses restricting the Indian partner's exports. As such clauses are rarely approved openly by government, foreign licensers have resorted to more subtle mechanisms of control like threatening to withhold supply of critical components, spareparts, etc., in case the Indian partner commences exporting products manufactured on licence. In most instances, it appears, the Indian partners accept clauses restricting their exports as part of a 'gentleman's agreement', written down in agreed minutes but not submitted for government approval.[41]

Notwithstanding these and other circumventions of Indian regulations pertaining to transfer of technology, it is our general impression that the combined effect of the regulatory framework developed during the 1970s has been a strengthening of the bargaining position of Indian licensees without seriously jeopardising the inflow of foreign technology. On the other hand, the successive 'liberalisations' since the mid-1970s probably have not brought about upgrading of Indian technology to the extent intended. This is not only due to reticence on the part of international technology suppliers, but also a result of insufficiently developed indigenous R & D infrastructure to absorb, adapt and develop the imported technology.

It appears that neither government nor private Indian companies assign appropriate priority to R & D. It is rather distressing that companies with foreign technical collaboration spend comparatively little on R & D. Several companies do not report any spending at all under this head. According to the RBI's fourth survey report on foreign collaboration in Indian industry, the total foreign exchange payments made on account of royalties, technical fees, etc., were considerably higher than the total revenue expenditure for R & D.[42] This is evidently inadequate by the standards of countries which have managed to absorb and adapt imported technology. In their case, the total R & D expenditure is generally a multiple of the money paid out for importing technology.[43]

Viewed in a wider context, Indian policies undoubtedly have contributed to reducing the country's technological dependence in two basic respects. If we conceive of technological dependence - and asymmetrical relations of power between suppliers and buyers in the international technology markets - as deriving from market imperfections, the effects of Indian policies may be interpreted as follows:[44] Firstly, they have contributed to reducing market imperfections based upon the lack of information about sources and terms of technology supply on the part of the Indian buyers. In addition to disseminating information regarding sources and terms of supply, the government has directly improved the buyers' negotiating positions by stipulating certain conditions for approving collaboration agreements, thus partly eliminating the effects of individual buyer's lack of information and knowledge. Secondly, the policies of the Indian government have contributed to reducing demand-determined market imperfections through strengthening of domestic R & D institutions, both public and - by means of concessions and fiscal incentives - private.[45] At the same time, however, the Indian government has not been able to affect in any significant way the market imperfections primarily based upon supply-side factors such as monopolistic or oligopolistic control over technology. This control may derive from superior know-how, investments in R & D, and innovation, but more often it is exercised by legal means, especially by taking out patents and by legal protection of trademarks.[46] These supply-determined market imperfections seem to have acquired relatively greater importance for Indian industry over the last decade. Precisely because the emphasis has been shifted to upgrading and acquisition of sophisticated technology, the number of potential suppliers has dwindled, quite often to a few TNCs. In a number of areas, this may easily have off-set the improvements attained with respect to market constraints determined by lack of information and demand factors, thus leaving Indian technology buyers with as little leverage and negotiating power as previously.

Notes and References

1. Implementation of FERA also brought down the number of foreign branches and subsidiaries. The number of branches declined from 540 in 1973/74 to 315 in 1979/80. The number of subsidiaries came down from 188 in the former year to 118 in the latter, the term 'subsidiary' here referring to a company incorporated in India with a majority of the equity shares held abroad by one share-holder. Cf. *Assocham Parliamentary Digest*, 1979, No. 4; and S. K.Goyal, *The New International Economic Order and Transnational Corporations*, op.cit., Table 1, p 7.The number of branches continued to decline after 1980. By 1984, an additional 60 branches presumably had stopped functioning while several others had converted themselves to Indian companies. Cf. Biswajit Dhar, *op.cit*.

2. *Statesman*, Calcutta, Feb. 17, 1977.

3. Cf., e.g., the concise discussion in World Bank, *World Development Report 1985*, London, Oxford University Press, 1985, p 125 ff.

Transfer of Resources 159

4. UNCTC, *Trends and Issues in Foreign Direct Investment and Related Flows*, New York, 1985, p 26 ff.

5. At the end of 1975, the stock of foreign investment amounted to US$ 2,400 million. By 1978, this figure had increased to US$ 2,500 million – a mere 4 per cent increase over three years. By 1981, the stock of direct OECD investment had climbed to US$ 2,700 million, i.e., an 8 per cent increase over 1978. Cf. OECD, *International Investment and Multinational Enterprises. Recent International Direct Investment Trends*, Paris, 1981, Table 9, p 46; and *Commerce*, April 16, 1983, p 668.

6. Cf. Chapter 1 above.

7. It may be noted in passing that this renewed interest was clearly manifested in several public statements issued by foreign business representatives. Almost as a rejoinder to Orville Freeman's statement, reproduced above, Craig Nalen, President of Overseas Private Investment Corporation, said in 1983: 'We recognize that no laws have changed, but we believe that a favourable investment climate exists.' *Business India*, May 9-22, 1983.

8. Including initial, further and bonus issues plus debenture issues and loans.

9. Cf. the RBI study mentioned as source for Table 5.4, p 84 f; and Government of India, Office of the Controller of Capital Issues, *Quarterly Statistics on the Working of Capital Issues Control*, Oct.-Dec.,1981, Statement 9, p 20.

10. It was only a question of accentuating a trend already noticable in India as well as in other LDCs. Cf. Charles Oman, op.cit.

11. See the second source referred to in note 9 above.

12. The list included such well-known corporations as Cola-Cola and IBM. Cf. *Assocham Parliamentary Digest*, 1981, No. 16, pp 70-71.

13. See India International Inc., *Doing Business Collaborations in India*, prepared for U.S. Department of State and the Overseas Private Investment Corporation, Washington, D.C., 1985, p 38 ff. The report states that American executives are 'relatively less sophisticated' than their competitors in their approach to India. More specifically, U.S. business executives are too impatient; many are not willing to make a long-term commitment to India, many are far too legalistic and inflexible, and some still insist on majority ownership rather than accepting guidelines. *Ibid.*, p 43.

14. Indo-American Chamber of Commerce, *Indo-U.S. Joint Ventures: Partners in Progress*, Bombay, 1982, p 3 f. It may be added that this study shows that the majority of American firms with joint ventures in India have experienced excellent growth in sales, profits and dividends. For the five-year period from 1976 to 1981, the annual average compound growth rates for 34 companies studied amounted to the following :

After-tax profits	20.3 per cent
Dividends	14.8 - -
Retained earnings	22.8 - -
Sales revenue	17.9 - -
Total assets	17.0 - -

    Such rates of growth ought not, according to the Chamber, deter any corporation from investing in India.

15. This observation is based on data in the information system of the Corporate Studies Group, Indian Institute of Public Administration. See also Biswajit Dhar, *op.cit.*, Annexure VII, which contains a list of companies with more than 10 per cent foreign equity holdings incorporated after 1984.

16. Sudip Chaudhuri, 'Financing of Growth of Transnational Corporations in India, 1956-75', *Economic and Political Weekly*, August 18, 1979.

17. Based on company annual reports and interviews with company executives in 1979 and 1983.

18. RBI, 'Trends in Consent for Issue of Capital....' *op.cit.*, Table 8, p 88.

19. *Ibid.*, Table 18, p 101.

20. *Economic Times*, November 20, 1983, referring to a study by the Economic and Scientific Research Foundation.

21. In only three months, the market price of 26 FERA companies' shares, issued during the five-year period 1979 to 1983, appreciated by around 174 per cent over their paid-up value as on June 30, 1983. Those of 425 non-FERA companies appreciated by only around 37 per cent. *Economic Times*, September 7, 1983, Mid-week review on 'Investment'.

22. M.Narayana Bhat, 'Equity Investment. Why is it declining lately?', *Economic Times*, November 12, 1983.

23. Cf. Subrata Roy, 'The Stock Markets: Up, Up and Away', *Business India*, July 29-August 11, 1985, p 114 ff.

24. The number of agreements submitted for approval varied between 427 and 450 over the four-year period 1975-1978. The number increased to 501 in 1979, reflecting the change referred to below. Information provided by the Ministry of Industry.

25. Cf. p 47 above. The shift was determined also by the higher priority now accorded to the export-led growth strategy which, among other things, required the Indian firms to become more competitive in international markets. This, in turn, presupposed import and adaptation of more foreign technology.

26. S.L.Kapur, op.cit., p 11, and information provided by Ministry of Industry.

27. It should be noted here that the initiative in an overwhelmingly large proportion of collaborations has been taken by Indian firms. This was also found in a study of 238 firms in EEC countries and 170 Indian enterprises engaged in collaboration with EEC firms; see L.Hoffman et al., *Technology Transfer and Investment. European Community - India*, Joint Report on the EC/India Project on the Problems and Perspectives of the Transfer of Technology between Firms in the European Community and India, Berlin, 1984.

28. A similar pattern was revealed in the study just referred to; see *ibid.*, p 4 ff., for a summary of the principal findings.

29. See, e.g., Bharat Bhushan, 'The New Deals', *Business India*, May 9-22, 1983; Meenakshi Behara, 'Welcome Back Yanks?', *Business India*, September 10-23, 1984; and *Economic Times*, June 6, 1984.

30. Year-wise data provided by Indian Investment Centre, New Delhi.

31. Based on information in Indian Investment Centre, *Directory of Foreign Collaborations in India: India-Japan*, Vol. IV A (1981-84), New Delhi, 1987.

32. See Table 6.2.

33. Cf. L.Hoffman et al., op.cit., p 2; and Sanjaya Lall & Sharif Mohannad, 'Multinationals in Indian Big Business', *Journal of Development Economics*, Vol. 13 (1983).

34. As regards the petrochemical industry this was shown in a study by Sushil Khanna: *Transnational Corporations and Technology Transfer: Contours of Dependence in the Indian Petrochemical Industry*, Calcutta, Indian Institute of Management, n.d.

(1982). Later published in *Economic and Political Weekly*, Annual number 1984. As regards the electronics industry, the difficulties became a matter of public concern when, in January 1984, two American and two European TNCs refused to participate in the manufacture of fourth generation computers. Cf. *Economic Times*, January 6, 1984.

35. After the backing-out of the four Western computer manufacturing corporations referred to in the previous note, the Indian government approached the Soviet Union. This country agreed to supply the latest generation of sophisticated computers. A few months later, Japan also agreed to supply such computers together with necessary training for servicing them. *Economic Times*, September 26, October 12, and December 4, 1984. A brief analysis of the development of India's computer industry is provided in Joseph M.Grieco, 'Between Dependence and Autonomy; India's Experience with the International Computer Industry', *International Organization*, Vol. 36, no. 3 (1982).

36. Cf. the discussion of previous examples of the application of this strategy in Chapter 2 above.

37. This was indicated also in a study which showed that for collaborations costing Rs. 150 crores, the cost of associated equipment import worked out to be around Rs. 1,000 crores per annum. *Economic Times*, April 22, 1984. See also Chapter 4 above.

38. Major changes in import policies may be inferred from RBI, 'Salient Features of the Import-Export Policy for 1980-81', *Reserve Bank of India Bulletin*, May 1980, pp 292-296; and policy explanations under the same heading in subsequent May issues of the *Bulletin*. The 'liberalizations' were to some extent forced upon the Indian government by the IMF as preconditions for the loan of SDR 5 billion which India obtained from the Fund in 1981. See Government of West Bengal, *The IMF Loan. Facts and Issues*, Calcutta, 1981.

39. A similar conclusion was reached in the abovementioned study of technology transfer from the European Community; cf. L.Hoffman *et.al.*, *op.cit.*, p 8.

40. See *ibid.*, p 8 f; and *Economic Times*, Dec..9, 1983, Other contractual aspects implying restrictions for the licensee are reviewed in S.L.Kapur, *op.cit.*, p 27 ff.

41. This was revealed during interviews in 1979 and 1983. Besides, I have had the opportunity to read several such 'classified' agreements. Some of these also contained other restrictive clauses not approved by government.
42. Cf. A.K.Bagchi, 'Foreign Collaboration in Indian Industry', *op.cit.*, p 917.
43. *Ibid.*, p 918.
44. This conception is derived from Sanjaya Lall's study, 'International Technology Market and Developing Countries', *Economic and Political Weekly*, Annual Number, February 1980, especially p 311 ff.
45. Among the more recent endeavours to strengthen domestic R & D should be emphasized government's decision to establish science and technology parks affiliated with major scientific institutions. Cf. Tyzoon T.Tyebjee, 'Catalysing Entrepreneurship and Innovation', *Business India,* January 14-27, 1985; and *Business India,* September 24 - October 7, 1984.
46. For a study of the effects of the Indian Patents Act, see A.K.Bagchi (in collaboration with P.Banerjee and U.K.Bhattacharya), 'Indian Patents Act and Its Relation to Technological Development in India', *Economic and Political Weekly*, February 18, 1984.

• CHAPTER 6 •

Effects of the Regulations on Allocation of Resources

In addition to controlling foreign exchange transactions and conserving foreign exchange resources, FERA aimed at influencing the sectoral allocation of capital and technology transferred to India The Act, furthermore, aimed at prompting foreign controlled companies to diversify their activities into certain sectors. Companies were permitted foreign equity shares above 40 per cent provided they engaged in production of items specified in a list of 19 priority industries open to foreign investment.[1] A closer scrutiny of this list reveals that most of the items included were basic intermediate goods and means of production necessary for India's further industrial development and, at the same time, in short supply in the country. Moreover, many of the products required sophisticated technology not available from indigenous sources. The list contained practically no consumer goods.

It is evident from these stipulations that FERA was designed with a view to squeezing out TNCs from consumer goods industries and into capital goods and basic intermediate goods, particularly those involving the application of sophisticated technology. In these respects, the FERA provisions reflected basic objectives of the more comprehensive industrial policies implemented through the industrial approval system, import regulations and, to some extent, the Reserve Bank's selective credit controls.

The major questions to be addressed on this background are, first, whether the sectoral allocation of resources transferred after 1974 tended to correspond with the stated objectives of the Indian government. Second, whether TNCs operating in India tended to diversify their activities in keeping with government priorities.

Prior to addressing these questions, however, it is appropriate to mention some immediate effects of the implementation of the FERA provisions relating to foreign equity participation. Most conspicuously, the number of foreign branches in insurance was brought down appreciably, from 55 in 1973/74 to 20 only two years later. Over the same period, the number of foreign branches in another low-priority industry, trade, declined from 69 to 63.[2] The number of branches in both these sectors continued to decline in subsequent years. Foreign controlled insurance and trade companies together with some other service companies accounted for the overwhelming majority of those directed by RBI to wind up or eliminate non-resident interest.[3]

As a result of government intervention, coupled with a large number of voluntary dilutions and mergers, foreign controlled firms exclusively engaged in non-banking services came to play an insignificant role after around 1982. It should be added, though, that in certain product lines, including some mass consumer goods, former foreign trading companies retained oligopolistic market positions. But they had, in the meantime, become vertically integrated with TNC subsidiaries primarily engaged in manufacturing.

Some foreign controlled consumer goods companies were also forced to - or opted to - wind up or eliminate non-resident interest. Most, however, continued to hold up to 40 per cent equity. A few of them retained even more than 40 per cent.[4] But overall, the enactment of the FERA provisions did reduce foreign presence and oligopolistic control in respect of consumer goods in general. However, as alluded to below, this conclusion did not apply to all branches within the consumer goods sector.

Sectoral Allocation of Foreign Capital and Technology

It is worth noticing at the outset that the sectoral distribution of foreign direct investment was in the process of change even prior to 1974. As can be gathered from Table 6.1, foreign investments in plantation and mining were on the decline in terms of their relative importance. Investments in services, which accounted for more than 40 per cent in 1948, had declined to around 17 per cent by 1961, but subsequently increased to 29 per cent. If insurance is left out, the latter increase was less spectacular. Trade played a continuously diminishing role for foreign investors. Investment in oil appreciated considerably during the 1950s, but then declined in terms of relative weight. After government's take-over of the major foreign oil companies in 1975, foreign investments in this sector were insignificant.

In contrast, foreign investments in manufacturing increased so rapidly that by 1974 this sector combined accounted for more than 55 per cent of all foreign investments in India. The relative importance of selected manufacturing industries is apparent from the Table.

After 1974, total outstanding long-term foreign liabilities continued to decline in relative terms in plantations, mining and petroleum. Those in services, on the other hand,

Table 6.1

Foreign Investment by Industry, 1948, 1961, 1974 and 1980

Percentage distribution

Industry	1948	1961	1974	1980-A	1980-B
Plantations	19.7	15.2	5.9	2.2	4.1
Mining	4.3	1.8	0.9	0.5	0.8
Petroleum	8.4	22.4	9.1	2.1	3.9
Manufacturing	26.7	43.3	55.2	49.2	87.0
– of which					
Foods, beverages, etc.	3.8	5.3	3.3	2.0	4.1
Textile products	10.6	3.1	3.5	2.4	3.4
Machinery, etc.[a]	5.7	20.1	19.8	21.0	36.3
Chemicals	3.0	7.9	21.1	17.8	32.3
Services	40.8	17.2	29.0	45.9	4.1
– of which					
Trading	16.3	4.3	1.8	1.1	2.2
Construction, utilities and transport	11.9	8.3	17.0	28.9	0.7
Financial[b]	5.9	1.8	9.3	15.2	0.5
Total	99.9	99.9	100.1	99.9	99.9

Note: Percentages under '1980-A' refer to total outstanding long-term foreign liabilities. These figures are comparable with those for previous years. Percentages under '1980-B' refer to investments in foreign branches and foreign controlled rupee companies.

a) Including transport equipment, machinery, machine tools, metals and metal products, electrical goods and machinery.

b) Foreign investments in insurance are not included in the figures for 1948 and 1961 but for 1974 and 1980.

Sources: Reserve Bank of India, *India's Foreign Liabilities and Assets. 1961-Survey Report*, Bombay 1964, Statement 9, p 71; RBI, 'India's International Investment Position, 1973-74', *Reserve Bank of India Bulletin*, March 1978, Statement IV, p 183; 'India's International Investment Position 1977-78 to 1979-80', *Reserve Bank of India Bulletin*, April 1985, Statement IV, p 291 f.

showed significant increase. By 1980, they accounted for almost 46 per cent of total foreign liabilities. Closer scrutiny, however, reveals that this latter change was due not to increased direct investment but to a marked increase in creditor liabilities. As may be inferred from the last column in Table 6.1, direct investment in services accounted for only 4.1 per cent in 1980, whereas investment in manufacturing in this sense accounted for not less than 87 per cent. A comparison with equivalent figures for previous years strongly supports the contention that investment in foreign branches and subsidiaries has been increasingly concentrated in manufacturing industries. Amongst these, the prime beneficiaries have been capital goods and basic intermediate industries, including industrial machinery, transport equipment and basic chemicals.[5]

This pattern in the sectoral allocation of foreign investments is not necessarily a result of the Indian government's policy, although in general the pattern is in keeping with that policy. The allocation may as well, and perhaps more likely, reflect the distribution of business opportunities, profitability ratios and growth prospects, i.e., conditions only marginally affected by government intervention.[6]

As regards the sectoral allocation of the foreign technology transferred to India we are obliged to employ as the prime indicator the number of foreign collaboration agreements entered into. This is a very crude indicator, but the only one allowing cross-sectoral comparisons.

Table 6.2 summarises available data on approved foreign collaborations by industry for the period 1970-1985.

According to the stated policy of the Indian

government, foreign collaboration has not been considered necessary, especially since 1978, in consumer goods industries listed in the Table - with the exception of ceramics.[7] The same policy principle has applied to several other industries, including paper and pulp, cement, glass, dyes and dyestuffs, and 25 pharmaceutical products.

Strict implementation of this policy would imply, if not an elimination of the industries concerned from the list of approved foreign collaborations, then at least a drastic reduction in the number of agreements approved. As can be inferred from the Table, this is not how the policy has been enforced. Actually, it is very difficult to discern any significant change whatsoever in the overall pattern of approvals by industry during the period studied.

Confronted with this evidence, highly placed government officials interviewed in 1983 explained the apparent absence of any policy impact by referring to three major circumstances. *First*, government never intended to rule out foreign technical collaboration with respect to products the manufacture of which did not require such collaboration, only to limit the costs of importing superfluous technology. Besides, some of the collaborations approved were, undoubtedly, parts of composite schemes involving manufacture of items requiring foreign technical assistance. *Second*, government did relax the policies pursued with regard to technology transfer before the original, and rather restrictive, stipulations were reflected in the statistics. The relaxation, however, was primarily in the implementation of policies, not in their formulation. *Third*, and most important, the simplified distribution of approved foreign collaboration agreements among industries enumerated in Table 6.2 con-

Table 6.2
Approved Foreign Collaborations – Industry-wise, Four-year Periods 1970–1985

	1970-73 Number	Percentage	1974-77 Number	Percentage	1978-81 Number	Percentage	1982-85 Number	Percentage
Industries producing primarily consumer goods	39	4.1	61	5.2	60	4.1	182	6.0
Textiles	9	0.9	12	1.0	13	0.9	25	0.8
Sugar	–	–	–	–	–	–	2	0.1
Fermentation industries	7	0.7	2	0.2	1	0.1	12	0.4
Food processing	2	0.2	10	0.9	8	0.5	22	0.7
Vegetable oil & vanaspati	–	–	1	0.1	1	0.1	1	0.0
Soaps, cosmetics & toilet preparations	–	–	2	0.2	2	0.1	6	0.2
Leather, leather goods	5	0.5	11	0.9	13	0.9	29	1.0
Cigarettes	–	–	–	–	–	–	–	–
Glue & gelatine	3	0.3	3	0.3	1	0.1	1	0.0
Ceramics	13	1.4	20	1.7	21	1.4	84	2.8
Chemical industries	106	11.2	145	12.4	156	10.5	294	9.7
Fertilizers	1	0.1	–	–	–	–	2	0.1
Chemicals other than fertilizers	94	9.9	136	11.6	142	9.5	253	8.3
Photographic raw film & paper	1	0.1	2	0.2	–	–	11	0.4
Dyestuffs	1	0.1	1	0.1	–	–	1	0.0
Drugs & pharmaceuticals	9	0.9	6	0.5	14	0.9	27	0.9

Allocation of Resources

Engineering	587	61.9	747	63.6	1025	68.8	2010	66.2
Boilers and steam generating plants	8	0.8	13	1.1	5	0.3	28	0.9
Electrical equipment and prime movers (4 & 5)	173	18.2	261	22.2	271	18.2	625	20.6
Telecommunications	5	0.5	-	-	23	1.5	53	1.7
Transportation and earth moving machinery (7 & 11)	84	8.9	88	7.5	116	7.8	263	8.7
Industrial machinery & machine tools (8 & 9)	237	25.0	305	26.0	481	32.3	651	21.4
Agricultural machinery	17	1.8	-	-	1	0.1	10	0.3
Mechanical & engineering misc. (12)	28	3.0	39	3.3	52	3.5	147	4.8
Industrial instruments and miscellaneous (13-17)	35	3.7	41	3.5	76	5.1	233	7.7
Other industries	216	22.8	221	18.8	248	16.7	549	18.1
Metallurgical industries (1)	45	4.7	61	5.2	72	4.8	148	4.9
Fuels (2)	1	0.1	2	0.2	10	0.7	33	1.1
Paper & pulp (24)	16	1.7	11	0.9	10	0.7	11	0.4
Rubber goods (30)	22	2.3	29	2.5	19	1.3	37	1.2
Glass (33)	13	1.4	17	1.4	17	1.1	33	1.1
Cement & gipsum products (35)	4	0.4	10	0.9	7	0.5	27	0.9
Consultancy	14	1.5	14	1.2	19	1.3	55	1.8
Miscellaneous industries (non-scheduled)	99	10.4	73	6.2	91	6.1	205	6.8
Total	948	100.0	1174	100.0	1489	100.0	3035	100.0

Sources: Indian Investment Centre, New Delhi.

Note: Figures in brackets refer to scheduled industry numbers in official documents. They are included only where necessary for unambiguous identifications.

ceals the fact that, generally speaking, a shift has occurred, away from low-technology areas towards production processes requiring sophisticated technology. Most of these relate to the manufacture of capital goods and basic intermediates. But some do relate to consumer goods and other industries of less strategic importance for reproduction.

On the basis of a closer scrutiny of details on technical collaborations approved since 1974[8] we tend to agree with this latter contention. Indeed, a shift appears to have taken place in the sense that collaboration agreements comprising transfer of sophisticated technology have become more frequent. Moreover, several of the agreements identified as belonging to 'closed' industries did involve transfer of at least some sophisticated know-how and capital-embodied technology. The major beneficiaries, however, were industries manufacturing industrial machinery, machine tools, industrial precision instruments, electronic components, computers, peripherals, telecommunication equipment, automotive ancillaries, and basic chemicals. These are all products the manufacture of which requires comparatively sophisticated technology.

In other words, the evidence lends some support to the official contention that government intervention has contributed to channelling foreign technology into capital goods and basic intermediate goods industries, particularly those involving application of sophisticated technology. Again, as with respect to capital flows, the changing pattern should perhaps be attributed just as much to changes in the distribution of business opportunities, etc. But at any rate, the sectoral and industry-wise allocation of foreign technology tended to change in keeping with government's stated objectives.[9]

Diversification of TNC Activities

By directing foreign controlled companies engaged in low-priority production for the domestic market to bring down non-resident interest to a maximum of 40 per cent, the Indian government expected subsidiaries of large TNCs to diversify their activities. By doing so, the companies could retain non-resident interest above the 40 per cent level, provided they diversified into high-priority manufacturing. Basically, this equity dilution strategy rested on the assumption that TNCs would normally prefer to retain a majority of voting shares or at least more than 40 per cent of voting shares in their Indian subsidiaries.

It is, however, difficult to find justification for this assumption. It is true that some TNCs have, as an integral part of their corporate strategy, preference for majority ownership. But more frequently TNCs are concerned much more with management control which they can easily retain with minority ownership. For instance, by diluting in the form of dispersing foreign shares or fresh equity widely among many individual shareholders, each with a small holding, effective control would remain with the foreign equity holder, even if this holder werein possession of, say, only 25 per cent voting shares. Whether disposing of holdings of foreign corporations or raising new capital from Indian capital market, the overwhelming majority of FERA companies chose to dilute foreign equity precisely by distributing their shares in widely dispersed lots, thus retaining full control over management.[10] Several FERA companies reinforced this strategy by allotting shares to employees of the companies, or by selling shares to various government financial institutions which would not ordinarily exercise their voting rights.[11]

In addition to securing continued effective managerial control by means of a commanding block of shares, several TNCs also have exercised control through specific long-term legal contracts. Such contracts, vesting control in the foreign party, have been inserted with the approval of the Indian government, even in cases where the foreign shareholder has held no more than 25 per cent of voting shares.[12]

Considering these – and possibly other methods by which TNCs compelled to reduce foreign equity holdings could maintain managerial control – there is no strong reason to expect the FERA provisions by themselves to squeeze out TNC subsidiaries from low-priority and into high-priority industries. But to the extent that the more encompassing industrial approval system was applied with the same objective, some diversification should be expected, because of the foreign controlled companies' dependence on government licences for expansion.

This particular dependence was what government attempted to exploit by discriminating against companies with more than 40 per cent foreign equity participation.[13] In addition to the general application of this discriminatory policy, government in 1978 and 1979 particularly requested some large TNCs to phase out their engagement in mass-consumption goods like soap, footwear, matches, chocolates, toothpaste and biscuits.[14] The licensing authorities did not, however, apply the full force of the approval system in all cases. Just as some of the powerful TNCs managed to get government permission to retain foreign shareholdings at levels above those stipulated in FERA,[15] so some of the larger corporations engaged in the manufacture of mass-consumption goods managed to obtain exceptional treatment.

Some TNC subsidiaries, apparently complying with government directives, at the same time established small-scale units in consumer goods industries in order to continue producing and selling in this profitable and growing market.[16]

Another response involved transfer of non-core sector activities to non-FERA, associated companies, thus increasing the percentage of core-sector activities within the concerned FERA companies. This, in turn, exempted these companies from equity dilution or diversification of activities.[17]

A third response implied the amalgamation of FERA companies primarily engaged in non-core sectors with companies already operating in core sectors, thus exempting the former from changing their allocation of resources.

In addition to permitting such — fully legal, but indisputable circumventions of the FERA provisions, the licensing authorities applied what could be termed a very liberal interpretation of the rules *vis-à-vis* certain particularly powerful TNCs, including Hindustan Lever.[18]

Although explicity directed to either dilute or phase out its production of soap in 1978, Hindustan Lever obtained necessary licences for considerable expansion of its soap manufacturing capacity. As a result, soap accounted for nearly 55 per cent of the company's total sales in 1984, compared with around 44 per cent in 1979.[19]

Several other examples of the 'pragmatism' and 'flexibility' with which the Indian government pursued its stated policies could be provided. It is of greater interest in this context, however, to take note of the fact that in spite of the 'lax' and selective implementation of the industrial licensing policies, the government did — under the circumstances prevailing — manage to pursuade several TNCs to diversify into core sectors. This even applied to Hindustan Lever which has diversified both vertically and horizontally.[20] Other corporations have pursued the same strategy.[21]

According to Indian government officials, this may be appreciated as a result primarily of government policies. According to some business representatives, the diversification and changing pattern of resource allocation should rather be interpreted as the most adequate corporate strategy under circumstances only marginally influenced by government policies and decisions.

Neither of these interpretations carry conviction. The former attributes too much importance to government policies, considering the many and varied options open to TNCs, especially those providing technology and products for which no local substitutes existed. The latter interpretation underestimates what could be termed the 'catalytic' impact of new government policies. The propensity on the part of TNCs operating in India to allocate resources to core sectors has been significantly higher after the enactment of FERA and associated regulatory policies than previously. Consequently, we favour an interpretation somewhere in between, according to which the new ownership rules and changed regulatory framework enacted after 1974 started, or at least speeded up, a diversification process. Several TNCs opted for dilution of equity rather than diversification. Others chose to increase exports without diversifying Some even preferred to close down their operations in India. But it still left a considerable number of comparatively large TNC-affiliated companies that 'turned adversity into opportunity'.[22] Instead of attempting to avoid the effects of the new regulations, they exploited them by successfully raising funds and obtaining licences and approvals for new product lines.

In this manner they diversified the risks associated with narrow product lines, limited production facilities and restricted markets. At the same time, new government licences obtained provided these TNCs with markets protected by effective entry barriers that kept out potential competitors, both foreign and Indian.[23]

Viewed in a wider perspective, the diversification of TNC activities into core industries, i.e., mostly industries of higher strategic importance for reproduction, has probably enhanced their overall economic power position and strengthened their bargaining power. Generally speaking, it should be easier for government to regulate activities of TNC subsidiaries producing mass-consumption goods like soft drinks or instant coffee than to regulate the activities of those producing, say, sophisticated machinery or basic industrial chemicals. The critical variable is, of course, not the use value and material characteristics of the products, but rather their strategic value to economic reproduction and the extent to which the products and the suppliers may be substituted. Other factors are important, too. The major point in the present context, however, is to emphasise that the diversifications which have taken place over the last decade have not reduced the extent of foreign control in Indian industry. On the contrary, these diversifications and the often associated backward and forward linkages have increased foreign influence in several industries of high strategic importance for reproduction, thereby simultaneously increasing their bargaining power *vis-à-vis* the Indian government.

In some industries, like the automotive tyre industry[24] or the manufacture of scooters and other two-wheelers, this tendency has been completely neutralised by the building up of

Indian controlled manufacturing capacities. In such cases, diversification has resulted in increased competition and import substitution, in keeping with government objectives.[25] But in other industries, like pharmaceuticals, basic chemicals and several engineering goods industries, foreign influence and control has clearly increased. It seems that, in addition to substituting imports, TNC subsidiaries have also substituted Indian industry - which was definitely not intended by government when designing the new regulatory framework. In a number of cases, TNC-affiliated companies have pre-empted growth opportunities by obtaining licences and establishing production before Indian industrialists could avail of the opportunities.[26] It even happened that foreign controlled companies managed to obtain permission to install capacities of such magnitudes that Indian companies were actually prevented from expanding into the product lines concerned.[27]

Summing up the effects of the post-1974 regulations on diversification of TNC activities, it seems warranted to conclude that the new policies did contribute to set in motion a re-allocation of TNC resources in favour of core industries. However, this re-allocation was carried out not primarily because of government regulations, but rather as a corporate response to favourable business opportunities in the said industries. By exploiting these opportunities to their own advantage, TNC affiliated companies in some cases simultaneously preempted growth opportunities and substituted local industry. This combined effect of TNC behaviour and the functioning of the industrial approval system was obviously not in keeping with government's stated policy objectives.

Notes and References

1. Cf. Appendix I.
2. CTC/ESCAP Unit, *Monitoring and Regulating Transnational Corporations in India*, op.cit., Table 1, p 52.
3. By 1982, the total number of companies directed to do so came to 97; see Table 3.2 above.
4. The extent of 'Indianisation' of foreign companies attained by early 1981 is shown for each registered company in *Assocham Parliamentary Digest*, 1981. No. 16 (14.9.1981-18.9.1981), pp 57-86.
5. This observation is supported by information regarding foreign investment provided in *Economic Times* since 1978. Although extensive in coverage, the data thus collected may not add up to a completely correct picture due to the way in which they have been selected. For instance, the business daily, understandably, has had a general preference for large individual investments.
6. It is of interest to note here that the sectors which have, over the last few years, attracted substantial foreign investment are among those with the highest growth rates during the last decade. Most TNC subsidiaries studied gave preference in their investment strategies to such sectors over those with high profitability ratios but with interior growth prospects See also the sector analyses in India International Inc., *Doing Business Collaborations in India*, op.cit., Part II.
7. Cf. Appendix II.
8. Details are provided quarterly as supplements to Indian Investment Centre's *Monthly Newsletter* as well as in *Economic Times*. For the purpose of the scrutiny referred to above we chose six three-month periods within the period 1976-1984. I have to admit, though, that my own technical knowledge is limited. Consequently, I had to rely on government's list of industries and items classified as requiring high technology.
9. At least one reservation is necessary here: not all the approved collaboration agreements were actually enforced. Consequently, the pattern with respect to the latter may deviate somewhat from the pattern identified above. Indeed, it appears that non-enforcement of agreements occurred more frequently with regard to transfer of high technology and upgrading than with regard to less sophisticated technical collaboration. An executive of one of the corporations which decided not to implement an approved agreement explained that, upon closer ana-

lysis the terms were found too restrictive and the financial returns too modest by the foreign partner. In spite of such occurrences, however, there is no reason to expect that they would create a pattern basically different from the one observed above.

10. A similar conclusion was reached in a comprehensive study of 12 selected TNCs; see Dennis Encarnation and Suchil Vachani, 'Foreign Ownership: When Hosts Change the Rules', *Harvard Business Review*, 1985, No. 5 (Sept.–Oct.), p 157.

11. This was emphasized also by A.K. Bagchi in his paper *Transnational Corporations as Transferors of Capital and Technology in India: Some Critical Issues*, Calcutta, Centre for Studies in Social Sciences, n.d. (1982), p 4 ff.

12. For illustrative examples, see S.K. Goyal, *Multinational Corporations in India: The Need for a Realistic Policy Framework*, New Delhi, Indian Institute of Public Administration, n.d. (1980).

13. Cf. the discussion in Chapter 3 above.

14. *Far Eastern Economic Review*, January 19, 1979, p 76. Hindustan Lever and WIMCO were specifically requested to phase out, within a period of three years, their production of soap and matches, respectively, and diversify their activities into core sectors.

15. Cf. p 178 ff, above.

16. Examples are provided in an illustrative list of TNCs with small-scale units in India in S.K. Goyal, *The New International Economic Order and Transnational Corporations*, op.cit., pp 19-20.

17. For examples, see *Business India*, July 4-17, 1983, p 50 ff.

18. Cf. p 179 ff, above.

19. Subrata Roy, 'Hindustan Lever: India's Largest Foreign Company', *Business India*, Sept. 23-Oct. 6, 1985; and *Business India*, July 21-Aug. 3, 1980, p 37.

20. See the articles referred to in the previous note. 'Vertical diversification' implies adding and combining stages of production processes in vertically integrated sequences of processing activities. 'Horizontal diversification' refers to addition of separate, unlinked production processes.

21. This is evident from a study of a large number of company annual reports, made available to me at the Indian Institute of Public Administration in 1983 and 1988. For published accounts, see, for

instance, R.N.Bhaskar, 'WIMCO's March beyond the Match', *Business India*, August 12-25, 1985, p 118 ff.; and Sushila Ravindranath, 'Pond's Aroma of Success', *Business India*, July 29-August 11, 1985.

22. The expression is used by Encarnation & Vachani, *op.cit.*, p 160.
23. Cf. *ibid.*, especially pp 154-158.
24. Cf. Sunil Mani, 'Concentration and Marketpower in Indian Automotive Tyre Industry', *Economic and Political Weekly*, May 25, 1985.
25. In the automotive tyre industry, a few large Indian business houses recently managed have to exploit horizontal and vertical integrations and collusive practices to the extent that they now hold oligopolistic positions in the market. See *ibid*. This does not, however, invalidate the above statement as a general rule, but it does indicate limits to its applicability with respect to market conditions.
26. Many TNC subsidiaries reaped great financial rewards from diversifying into new sectors. This is evident from their annual reports. See also Encarnation & Vachani, *op.cit.*, p 157 ff.; and the articles referred to in notes 19 and 21 above.
27. Instances were mentioned by both government officials and Indian business representatives during interviews in 1979 and 1983. The strongest criticism, however, was advanced by executives of public sector companies who complained that government often favoured foreign corporations over Indian state enterprises. Public attention has been drawn especially to government's licensing policies with regard to fertilizers.

• CHAPTER 7 •

Summary and Discussion of Findings

This concluding Chapter contains a synopsis of the major findings of our investigation and analysis. Besides, these findings are discussed, albeit rather briefly, within broader contexts with a view to ascertaining essential determinants for effective control of TNC activities in less developed countries.

Less Developed Countries and Transnational Corporations

In their relations with TNCs, less developed countries (LDCs) are caught in a dilemma. On the one hand, TNCs can provide these countries with scarce capital resources, sophisticated technology, management skills and employment opportunities. Furthermore, TNCs command access to superior global distribution and marketing systems. They may thus offer opportunities for increasing exports. On the other hand, it is commonly acknowledged that TNCs do not necessarily provide capital, technology, employment opportunities or access to global distribution and marketing facilities to any great extent. And when they do so, it often inflicts on less developed host countries excessively high costs, because the corporations may take advantage of their monopolistic or oligopolistic positions. At any rate, TNCs frequently cause distortions in less developed host countries' economic systems and reduce the effectiveness of national development programmes and economic policies (p 20 ff).

Whether costs and disadvantages associated with TNC operations prevail over benefits cannot be ascertained *a priori*. It depends on several factors, the most influential of which relate to conditions of capital accumulation, growth potential and long-term profit maximisation in a national as well as global perspective (p 21 ff).

Under certain conditions, sizable net benefits may indeed accrue to LDCs, even from TNC operations shaped by considerations of short-term profit maximisation and rapid growth. But – and this is the major point here – TNC behaviour is not determined by branches or subsidiaries in LDCs. Corporate strategy and behaviour are determined primarily by the parent company. More specifically, the whole question of how and where resources and skills are allocated and utilised within a transnational corporation is decided on the basis of the parent company's interests, not on the basis of those of the branches or subsidiaries. In this sense, looked at from the point of view of less developed host countries, the processes of resource circulation, capital accumulation and deployment of technology and skills within TNCs are, to a great extent, externally determined (p 24 f).

From this perspective, it becomes quite obvious that indigenous social forces in these countries have an interest in establishing some sort of control over TNC operations.

Host Government Regulations

The major problems facing policy-makers in India – as in other LDCs – are essentially how to 'manipulate societal conditions in such a way that TNCs are forced into, or acquire an interest in, sustaining and accelerating the country's internally-oriented economic development. More specifically, the policymakers must induce the corporations to provide larger financial resources, more adequate technology at lower costs, access to global distribution and marketing systems, and other resources in the broadest sense of the term. Furthermore, it is a question of how to influence the flows of capital, technology, and other resources to the maximum benefit of the host country's economic development (p 26 ff).

It is worthy of note that with this conception, regulation cannot be reduced to limiting TNC activities as much as possible. In a wider sense, the terms 'regulation' and 'control' denote government interventions which produce, or at least intend to produce, a higher degree of internally-oriented economic development. In a narrow sense, the terms refer to interventions which aim at maximising gains and minimising costs from TNC operations. In either case, endeavours aimed at limiting TNC activities should be confined to those with no positive net effects, perhaps even to those with no potential positive net effects.

The government of a host country may apply four overall and interrelated strategies in order to increase net benefits from TNC operations (p 32 f)

First, the government may intervene in a manner that renders superfluous specific TNC activities. This strategy may be pursued either by supporting expansion of private indigenous business at the expense of TNCs, or by establishing public sector undertakings to replace TNC operations.

Second, the government may contribute to

augmenting the attractiveness of the country as a host for TNCs. This may be done by improving certain basic economic and social conditions, including infrastructure, or by changing politically determined incentives in favour of TNCs.

Third, the government can enact specific regulations and restrictions (in the narrow sense) with a view to minimising costs and disadvantages from TNC activities, and at the same time maximising gains and benefits.

Fourth, the government of a host country can help rendering superfluous its own regulations by supporting indigenous business houses and improving their negotiating position *vis-à-vis* TNCs.

Indian Policies Affecting Transnational Corporations

Chapter 2 of this study contains a systematic description of Indian policies affecting the operations of TNCs. In addition to an account of legislation and rules relating specifically to foreign private investments and transfer of technology, this comprises a discussion of government interventions coming under the heading of the four strategies just outlined.

The policies discussed are analysed and evaluated primarily in terms of effectiveness, i.e., the degree to which they contribute to achieving or maintaining stated objectives. The other is the set of objectives implicit in sets of objectives. One is the set of objectives referred to in official policy declarations. Another is the set of objectives implicit in the theoretical model of internally-oriented industrial development.

In subsequent chapters the policies are also, to some extent, judged in terms of efficiency. As a concept, this refers to the quantity of resources expended – or the opportunities foregone – in the effort to achieve stated objectives. The major problem involved here is the difficulty of ascertaining costs, including opportunity costs, arising from the policies pursued. Consequently, the criterion of efficiency can not be applied in a strict and quantified manner.

A third criterion which guides the analyses and assessment is responsiveness. This refers to the authorities' ability to respond to changing economic conditions and rearrangement of priorities.

We shall briefly summarise the discussion of policies related to the first and third strategy in the above enumeration.

Rendering Superfluous TNC Activities

The Indian government has contributed to reducing the country's dependence on TNCs by replacing their activities through the establishment and enlargement of public sector undertakings. Government's policy towards the oil industry provides a good illustration.

In the two decades after independence, control of the oil industry in India lay overwhelmingly with a few large transnational oil corporations. The authorities tried in various ways to induce these corporations to operate in keeping with stated policy objectives, but generally in vain. Not until government, by the mid-1970s, had established competing public sector refineries, distribution systems, etc., did it succeed in acquiring control over this vital economic sector (p 41 ff). The ultimate outcome of the confrontation over oil was an almost complete elimination of the major foreign oil corporations and fairly effective regulation of other foreign enterprises engaged in this industry.

A similar approach was applied in relation to other industries, although not as systematically and persistently as in the case of the oil industry.

The general conclusion drawn from the Indian experience must, however, be viewed in a wider context. As mentioned in Chapter 1, there has been an increased willingness on the part of TNCs in general to alter their involvement from direct investment in wholly owned or majority owned subsidiaries to other forms of involvement. This major change has been particularly pronounced in the oil industry. In other words, the specific developments in India more or less coincided with dominant trends of adjustment in corporate strategies.

These strategies have undoubtedly been influenced by LDC government policies, including those of the Indian government. Nevertheless, the above observation leaves the impression that the struggle for control over equity in the oil sector was won by the Indian authorities partly because corporate strategies had changed.

Policies Governing Foreign Investments and Transfer of Technology

With respect to the third type of state interventions, i.e., specific regulations and restrictions which aim for a surplus of benefits over costs and disadvantages from TNC operations, India has developed a comprehensive and integrated system of controls, especially since 1969.

The central piece of legislation affecting TNCs in India was the Foreign Exchange Regulation Act (FERA), which was promulgated in 1973. It came into force on January 1, 1974.

Section 29 of this Act referred directly to

TNCs and other foreign companies operating in India. According to the Section, all non-banking foreign branches and subsidiaries with non-resident equity shares exceeding 40 per cent had to obtain permission from the Reserve Bank of India to carry on with business in the country. They also had to obtain specific approval to establish new undertakings, to purchase shares in existing companies, or to acquire, wholly or partly, any other company. Guidelines for administering Section 29 were announced in December 1973, and later amended in 1976.

According to the revised guidelines, all branches of foreign companies should convert themselves into Indian companies with at least 60 per cent local equity participation. Furthermore, all subsidiaries should bring down their foreign equity share to 40 per cent or less. Excempted from these rules were, however, companies exporting a substantial part of their production and companies engaged in core sectors and priority industries. In these cases, the guidelines provided for higher levels of foreign equity (pp 49 f, 67 f).

These exceptions to the general rule reflected government's endeavours to induce TNCs to use their superior access to global distribution and marketing systems, with a further view to improving India's balance-of-payments position. Besides, they reflected a desire on the part of the Indian government to channel TNCs away from certain industries and into core sectors and high priority industries. The latter included primarily basic intermediates and capital goods, whereas the former group comprised mainly consumer goods. As a rule, the manufacture of priority items required sophisticated technology not available from indigenous sources (pp 50 f, 54 f).

After the enactment of FERA, the regulatory

framework relating to TNC investments in India comprised five major acts and rules framed thereunder. The most important of the acts were the Industries (Development and Regulation) Act of 1951, the Monopolies and Restrictive Trade Practices Act of 1969, and FERA of 1973.

A review and comparison of the coverage of these acts revealed that not all foreign controlled companies came under the purview of the combined regulatory framework (p 51 ff). As pointed out later in the study, the loopholes permitting TNC subsidiaries to avoid government restrictions, e.g., by establishing small-scale affiliates, were exploited by some corporations.

In addition to the account of policies governing foreign investments in India in general, Chapter 2 also reviews the terms on which foreign corporations have been permitted to enter into technical collaboration agreements (p 54 ff).

These terms have become more and more specific since 1969. Besides, the policies governing transfer of technology have been integrated into the overall regulatory framework pertaining to foreign participation in India's economic development. The long-term goal of promoting technological self-reliance has remained the same within this new framework. But the emphasis has shifted from the principle of 'indigenous availability' to that of 'the necessity for continued inflow of technology in sophisticated and high priority areas'. At the same time, the new guidelines focus on how to bring down the costs of necessary technological imports.

Proclaimed Policies and Their Implementation and Effects

The review in Chapter 2 of Indian policies focuses on stated objectives and intentions. The subsequent investigation of the implementation in Chapter 3 focuses on possible discrepancies between the proclaimed policies and the policies actually pursued. The latter are, in turn, analytically separated from the analyses of effects and impacts brought about by decisions taken and policies pursued. These analyses are presented in Chapters 4 through 6.

It is the implementation and effects of the third type of state interventions which are the chief objects of the present study. In particular, the study is concerned with how the policies directly affecting TNC activities have been administered and implemented in the period since 1974. Subsequently, the study reveals how the regulatory framework, developed by 1974, has influenced the activities and impact of TNCs in selected respects.

Administration and Implementation of Indian Policies

Chapter 3 surveys the administration of Indian policies towards foreign investments. The survey includes a description of the administration of the industrial approval system. The Chapter also discusses the implementation of FERA directives issued pursuant to Section 29, i.e., those stipulating dilution of foreign equity holdings. Finally, the Chapter provides a brief outline of the actual functioning of the industrial approval system vis-à-vis TNC-affiliated companies.

Implementation of Section 29 of FERA

Our investigation of the implementation of

the equity dilution provisions enacted after 1974 reveals that, by June 1979, more than 95 per cent of the applications received had been finally disposed of. This shows both willingness and ability on the part of implementing institutions to make decisions in pursuance of government policy in this area.

However, if we consider more closely the enforcement of decisions where equity dilution was involved, a somewhat different pattern emerges. By June 1979, only 54 per cent of the companies directed to dilute had carried out the process as stipulated. Most of the companies concerned were in the process of diluting, but 64 had yet to initiate the process. Not until 1982, i.e., eight years after FERA came into force, did the last group of 28 companies receive final directives issued pursuant to the Act (p 71 ff).

An account of the decisions taken by RBI and the FERA Committee up to the end of 1985 showed that a total of 252 foreign controlled companies were exempted from the general rule stipulating a maximum of 40 per cent non-resident interest (p 74 ff). There is no doubt that most of these companies qualified for exemption in accordance with the FERA guidelines. But, as a closer scrutiny revealed, there is reason to doubt that they all qualified.

Almost all the companies exempted belonged to only three groups: they were either engaged in tea plantation activities or in the manufacture of drugs and pharmaceuticals, or they were affiliated with particularly large and powerful TNCs.

Companies engaged in tea plantations qualified for special treatment ever since FERA was enacted, in the sense that tea plantations were to be treated on par with 'core industries'. This was explained by government officials with reference to the importance of tea in India's foreign trade and the country's dependence on transnational tea companies for marketing Indian tea under their brand names. In other words, it appears that the interests of foreign tea companies were 'built into' the Indian economy to such an extent that they could strongly influence the decision-making processes already at the policy formulation stage. It was, therefore, not necessary for these companies to oppose the implementation of the policies (p 75 ff).

Companies engaged in the manufacture of drugs and pharmaceuticals did not qualify for exceptional or preferential treatment as a group. Nevertheless, a number of TNCs in this industry managed to prevent the implementation of FERA provisions regarding equity dilution as long as they had a vital interest in doing so (p 76 ff). India was very much dependent on transnational pharmaceutical corporations for supply of several bulk drugs, drug intermediates and even essential formulations. Under these circumstances, decision-makers in government abstained from applying the FERA provisions on these companies for fear of provoking a closing down of their operations in India. This would force the country to import the drugs concerned from essentially the same corporations, probably at higher prices and in foreign currency. It was quite obvious, therefore, that should the government succeed in acquiring effective control over the industry, it had to build up parallel indigenous capacity – according to principles similar to those applied earlier with respect to the oil industry. This was fully recognised by influential decision-makers when, in 1978, a new policy on drugs and pharmaceuticals was formulated (p 82 f).

The Indian government did not acquire effective control over the drugs and pharmaceuticals industry during the period studied. But it is probably justified to conclude that the expanded indigenous capacity allowed government to put more pressure on FERA companies within the sector by means of withholding industrial approvals (p 82). It should be added, however, that these possibilities were not utilised optimally by the policy implementing agencies due to mutual disagreement and conflict. It should also be added that the conditions for equity dilution were at the same time changed in such a way that transnational pharmaceutical companies had no longer reasons to fear losing management control as a consequence of giving up majority control over equity (p 79 f). In other words, their vital interest in thwarting implementation of FERA had weakened appreciably.

The third group of TNCs which managed to delay and distort the implementation of the new equity dilution rules comprised only a few, but very powerful corporations. They were able to secure for themselves most 'liberal' interpretations of the FERA guidelines when the government determined permissible levels of foreign equity participation. Criteria not included in the guidelines were introduced on an *ad hoc* basis in order to meet demands from powerful corporations for higher foreign equity levels (p 83 ff).

The review of the functioning of the industrial approval system indicates that the implementation of Indian licensing policies did not in any significant way restrict the expansion and activities of TNC-affiliated companies in general (p 87 ff). The system probably functioned as a disincentive to potential investors, discouraging TNCs unfamiliar with the country and its economic policies. This possibly inflicted net costs and disadvantages upon India (p 91 f). The approval system may also have acted as a disincentive to some TNCs already operating in India. Executives of smaller subsidiaries and those of newly established foreign controlled companies generally expressed great dissatisfaction with the approval system. The same applied to a few larger companies. But in these latter cases, it appears to be the result primarily of chosen corporate strategies, rather than a 'rational' and optimising response to Indian industrial licensing policies. As regards the overwhelming majority of large, established and experienced TNC-affiliated companies, they were able to extract sizable benefits from the working of the approval system, not necessarily in keeping with government policy. In other words, the approval system proved ineffective as a regulatory framework in relation to resourceful TNCs which chose to come to terms with the system.

The ineffectiveness and inefficiency of the approval system was due partly to loopholes in the legislation governing foreign economic engagement in India (pp 51 ff, 92). Besides, the 'political will' has fluctuated, to say the least, over the last decade when it came to implementing the stipulations contained in acts and policy statements. Furthermore, lack of administrative ability undoubtedly contributed to the ineffectiveness of the system. The implementing agencies were not equipped to cope with the far-reaching discretionary authority delegated to them. Consequently, this aspect of the system has generally strengthened the negotiating position of large TNC-affiliated companies, primarily because of their superior technical knowledge (pp 86, 92; and Chapter 5).

Effects of the Regulations on India's Balance of Payments

The strategy and objectives embodied in FERA relate to the distribution of equity and remittance of profits in the form of dividends. It was, therefore, considered expedient to commence the analysis of effects by taking a closer look, in Chapter 4, at the equity dilution process and its impact on dividend remittances abroad. Then follows a discussion of the assumption on which the equity dilution strategy has been based. TNC responses to the new regulatory framework are investigated with respect to profit remittances, expenditure in foreign currency in general, and exports. On this basis, the direct effects on India's balance of payments from TNC operations are studied in the last section of the Chapter.

Effects on the Remittance of Dividends

FERA aimed at regulating foreign exchange transactions with a further view to conserving foreign exchange resources and the proper utilisation thereof in the interest of India's economic development. The equity dilution strategy adopted to achieve this aim was based on the assumption that a reduction in foreign equity participation would automatically bring about a reduction in remittances abroad (p 98 f). More specifically, it was expected that the reduction in foreign equity participation would appear as an overall decrease in dividends paid abroad as a percentage of total dividends paid.

At variance with this expectation, our investigation actually reveals that the share of dividends paid abroad increased to a peak of around 20 per cent in the late 1970s. Even by 1983, the drain on foreign exchange resources on account of dividend remittances had not, after several years of equity dilution, been brought down below the level prevailing in 1975-76 (p 101 ff).

Dividend and Other Remittances

During the period studied, dividend remittances constituted only a minor share of total foreign exchange utilisation. The bulk of the outgo was on account of imports. This applied to both foreign and Indian controlled enterprises (p 111 ff).

Technical payments increased significantly after 1974. In several industries they became more important than dividend remittances. The tendency was accentuated by changing preferences on the part of TNCs in favour of so-called new forms of investment involving no or only minority financial participation. Foreign minority-owned firms showed an appreciably higher propensity than foreign majority-owned companies for remitting 'economic profits' in the form of technical payments (pp 110, 115 ff).

The equity dilution process, initiated by the FERA regulations, directly affected the overall remittance pattern, in the sense that they brought about an increase in the relative share of foreign minority-owned companies and, consequently, an increase in the relative share of technical payments. Otherwise, FERA did not substantially change the pattern of foreign exchange utilisation during the period studied, i.e., up to the mid-1980s.

The data analysed showed a marked difference between foreign controlled and Indian companies with respect to expenditure in foreign currency. It should be expected, perhaps, that foreign controlled companies remit comparatively higher sums on account of dividends, technical payments, etc. What is less obvious is that they should also import substantially more than their Indian counterparts in proportion to total income, sales and consumption. This is nevertheless what the study indicates. Neither FERA, nor the more comprehensive regulatory framework, had any discernible impact on TNC-affiliated or other foreign controlled companies' 'higher propensity to import' (p 118 ff).

What is even more disturbing, perhaps, is the revealed tendency among foreign controlled companies to import increasingly higher proportions of raw materials, components, stores and spares consumed (p 121 f).

Effects on the Balance of Payments

The fact that the import content for companies with close foreign connections tend to be higher than that for other companies need not necessarily imply that they inflict a net loss on India. They could easily balance or offset the outgo in foreign currency by exporting and thus earning equivalent amounts.

However, foreign controlled companies in general did not apply their superior global distribution and marketing systems in order to enhance exports from India. In this respect, neither FERA nor government's export promotion policies brought about the effects intended (pp 123 f, 127 ff). Recently published data even show a decline in the export performance of foreign controlled companies.

It is interesting to note that most of the TNC executives interviewed explained the relatively low export performance by referring to the fact that they had come to India not in order to produce for exports, but to take advantage of the growing domestic market.

The total impact of the private corporate sector on India's balance of payments turned negative during the period studied. This was in open contradiction with the official policy of import substitution and export expansion. Paradoxically, FERA and the industrial licensing policies may have contributed to the unintended evolution. This could be the case because the said policies have acted as pressures on foreign companies to bring down their engagement in consumer goods industries, where they had extensive export potentials. Instead, they were impelled to expand their operations in engineering and chemicals, where they had neither an interest in nor the same potential for export.

At the same time, certain aspects of the export promotion policies worked against attaining the objectives embodied in FERA and the industrial approval system. This is so, in particular, with respect to the concessions given to 'Export Houses' and 'Trading Houses'. Several TNC-affiliated companies managed to get themselves registered under these schemes, thus securing for themselves exceptional treatment. The manner in which they have obtained status as 'Export Houses' or 'Trading Houses' was often such that they could only be characterised as exploitation of loopholes in the regulatory framework. The major point here, however, is that the export promotion policies pursued by the Indian government were not all properly coordinated with the policy framework aimed at extracting the maximum net benefits from TNC operations (p 126).

Effects of the Regulations on Transfer of Resources

The policies pursued after 1974 were not intended to affect the inflow of foreign capital and technology. If anything, they should have stimulated these inflows. Besides, the regulations were framed in such a manner that foreign companies were impelled to channel their investible resources and technology in accordance with priorities fixed in Indian development plans.

Chapter 5 focuses on possible influences of the post-1974 regulations on the flows of foreign capital and technology. Sectoral allocations and diversification of activities are considered in Chapter 6.

Effects on Provision of Capital

The data analysed in Chapter 5 indicate that FERA did affect the provision of foreign capital: directly, by prompting some foreign corporations to disinvest; indirectly, by deterring several others from investing in India (p 139 ff). The flow of foreign direct investment to India declined drastically in the three-year period after 1975. A transitory increase after 1977 was replaced, in 1981, by another contraction. Only a minor part of this latter decline, however, can be attributed to conditions prevailing in India (p 140 ff). The decline after 1981 was associated with increased foreign involvement through minority equity participation and technical collaboration agreements.

Consequently, the importance of foreign direct investments continued to decline relative to non-equity forms of collaboration. The implementation of the new equity provisions directly contributed to bringing down rather drastically foreign participation in corporate capital formation (p 146 ff). Viewed in a broader perspective, FERA accentuated the general tendency toward reducing the importance of majority-owned foreign controlled companies in India.

The declining importance of foreign sources

in the financing of corporate growth implied that the foreign exchange leakages referred to in Chapter 4 were to a diminishing extent off-set by provision of foreign equity capital. At the same time, it appears that FERA companies, by enlisting local capital preempted scarce capital resources and crowded out potential Indian borrowers (p 149 ff). It should be added, though, that the extensive selling of stock in India by well-known, financially secure and profitable TNC affiliates simultaneously contributed to developing the country's capital market institutions. Consequently, the crowding out of potential Indian borrowers was noticeable primarily during the late 1970s.

Effects on Provision of Technology

The enactment of the FERA provisions regarding foreign equity participation only marginally affected the inflow of foreign technology. But the integration of the controls governing this inflow into the overall regulatory framework pertaining to foreign participation in India's economic development did affect the inflow, especially during the period 1975-1979. Again, the set-back was only transitory, however. Minor changes in the policies pursued and in related administrative procedures brought about a more favourable response from international technology suppliers (p 153 ff). As a result, the number of foreign collaboration agreements concluded increased significantly after 1979. A country-wise breakup shows a remarkable increase in the number of collaboration agreements concluded with Japanese companies after 1981.

In spite of these developments, it remained a serious problem throughout the period studied that technology suppliers showed strong reticence when it came to providing advanced technology. Several Indian firms in both the public and the private sector have experienced difficulties obtaining access to updated, advanced technology. And when such technology has actually been procured, the licensees have often not been able to obtain required technical support from the suppliers (p 157 ff).

A closer scrutiny revealed that this reticence on the part of international technology suppliers could not be explained primarily with reference to Indian policies. A more important determinant appeared to be the fear that Indian industry might be able to exploit the technologies transferred for increasing exports in direct competition with the licensers concerned (p 158 ff).

Apart from the difficulties associated with the procurement of certain sophisticated technologies and technical support, Indian purchasers of foreign know-how and technology have experienced some improvement over the last decade. Their bargaining positions have generally been strengthened, especially with respect to cost reductions, avoidance of undesirable and restrictive clauses, and unpackaging of technology.

Viewed in a wider context, Indian policies have without doubt, contributed to reducing the country's technological dependence in certain basic respects (p 161 f). At the same time, however, the Indian government has not been able to affect the monopolistic or oligopolistic nature of global technology markets. These supply-determined market imperfections seem to have acquired relatively greater importance for Indian industry over the last decade. Precisely because the emphasis has been shifted to upgrading and acquisition of sophisticated technology, the number of potential suppliers have dwindled even further. This may easily have off-set other improvements attained, thus leaving Indian technology buyers with as little leverage and negotiating power as previously.

Effects of the Regulations on Allocation of Resources

In addition to controlling foreign exchange transactions, FERA aimed at influencing the sectoral allocation of capital and technology transferred to India. The Act, furthermore, aimed at squeezing out TNCs from consumer goods industries and inducing them to diversify their activities into capital goods and intermediate goods industries.

Evidence presented in Chapter 6 shows that, generally speaking, the enactment of FERA did reduce foreign presence and oligopolistic control in respect of consumer goods. Besides, it appears that government intervention has contributed to channelling foreign capital and technology into capital goods and basic intermediate goods, particularly those involving application of sophisticated technology. There is some doubt, however, as to whether the changing pattern should be attributed just as much to changes in the distribution of business opportunities, profitability ratios and growth prospects. But at any rate, the sectoral and industry-wise allocation of foreign capital and technology tended to change in keeping with government's stated objectives (p 171 ff).

Diversification of TNC Activities

By directing foreign controlled companies engaged in low-priority production for the domestic market to bring down non-resident interest to a maximum of 40 per cent, the Indian government expected subsidiaries of TNCs to diversify their activities. This was based on the assumption that TNCs would normally prefer to retain more than 40 per cent of voting shares.

Closer scrutiny, however, revealed that this applies only to a minority of TNCs. More frequently they are concerned with management control which they can retain with even very small blocks of voting shares. In most cases, therefore, the FERA provisions by themselves did not effectively induce TNCs to transfer resources from low-priority industries into high-priority industries. But to the extent that the more encompassing industrial approval system was applied with the same objective, the new policies did contribute to set in motion a reallocation of TNC resources in favour of core industries. As concluded in Chapter 6, this reallocation was in many cases carried out not primarily because of government regulations, but rather as a corporate response to favourable business opportunities in the said industries (p 180 ff).

By exploiting these opportunities to their own advantage, TNC-affiliated companies in some cases simultaneously preempted growth opportunities and substituted local industry. This was obviously not in keeping with government's stated policy objectives.

Viewed in a wider perspective, the diversification of TNC activities into core sectors, i.e., mostly industries of higher strategic importance for reproduction, has probably not reduced the extent of foreign control in Indian industry. On the contrary, these diversifications and the often associated backward and forward linkages have increased foreign influence in several industries, thereby also increasing their bargaining power vis-à-vis the Indian authorities and private companies.

Concluding and Generalising Comments

The problems facing host country authorities are essentially how to 'manipulate' societal conditions in such a manner that TNCs are induced to providing larger financial resources, more adequate technology at lower costs, access to global distribution and marketing systems, and other resources in the broadest sense of the term. In addition, it is a question of how to influence the flows of capital, technology and other resources in ways conducive to furthering and strengthening the internally-oriented industrial development.

As shown in this book, the Indian authorities have succeeded only to a limited extent in these terms. It is evident that there is still considerable scope for improvements in India's policies towards TNCs. Compared with other LDCs, however, the results attained are relatively impressive. The same applies when we compare the Indian Government's performance prior to 1969 with the policy impact since 1974, the period 1969-74 being transitory and marked by shifting and indistinct impacts of state interventions.

The improvements and more effective control over TNC activities were brought about primarily through coordinated implementation of two major strategies. One implied the establishment and expansion of public sector undertakings to compete with or replace TNC operations. The other strategy implied enactment of specific regulations and restrictions with a view to minimising costs and disadvantages from TNC activities, simultaneously extracting maximum gains and benefits from these activities. It should be added that the most effective component of the policies pursued in accordance with the latter strategy was not the FERA regulations, but rather the more encompassing industrial licensing policies.

It is evident that the strategies evolved after 1969 affected TNC operations to the extent ascertained primarily because of associated improvements in the institutional set-up through which the new regulatory policies were implemented. It is even more important, however, that the introduction of new policies and modified institutional arrangements coincided with basic changes in India's socio-economic structures. During the decade after 1965, the indigenously controlled industrial base was significantly expanded not only in consumer goods industries but also in those manufacturing capital goods and basic intermediates. Concurrently, India's dependence on inflow of capital and machinery lessened. Indian industry even managed to diversify exports in favour of capital goods and basic intermediates. Partly as a result of these and other basic changes, and partly reinforced by political initiatives and improved organisation of Indian business, the whole environment turned more conducive to effective regulation of TNC activities. In comparison with preceding decades, and presumably in comparison with almost all other LDCs, the basic economic and social conditions thus allowed for the implementation of relatively advanced and effective regulatory measures aimed at consolidating and furthering internally-oriented industrial development.

This does not imply, though, that the Indian government, when acting on its own or in conjunction with Indian business, can do so independently of foreign capital interests. As pointed out above, recent developments, especially as a consequence of TNC diversifications into core sectors, may even have increased the impact of foreign capital interests in industrial branches of strategic importance for national development. This tendency may have been further accentuated during the 1980s as a result of the Indian government's stronger emphasis on an export-led growth strategy. The success of this strategy depends to an appreciable extent on the willingness of TNCs to cooperate with Indian business in terms of technology transfer and provision of access to global distribution and marketing systems.

The process toward more effective control over TNC activities in India is, therefore, not necessarily irreversible. Further analyses are needed in order to identify the critical variables in the long-term process of interaction between TNCs and less developed host countries. The present study has confined itself primarily to identifying problems and deficiencies in India's post-1974 regulatory framework in a short-term perspective. It is hoped, however, that this investigation may add to the general understanding of the processes and problems involved in LDC goverment's regulations of TNC operations.

Appendices

Appendix I: Priority Industries Open to Foreign Investment

According to a policy statement of February 1973, foreign concerns and affiliated companies of foreign concerns are eligible to participate in the industries specified in the list below along with other applicants. They will ordinarily be excluded from the industries not included in this list.

The list of industries, known as Appendix I-industries, was revised in 1982. The revised list is reproduced below. It is worth noting that the revised list is much more precise and operational.

Appendix I-Industries, 1973-1982

1. Metallurgical Industries
   (1) Ferro alloys
   (2) Steel castings and forgings
   (3) Special steels
   (4) Non-ferrous metals and their alloys
2. Boilers and Steam Generating Plants
3. Prime Movers (other than Electrical Generators)
   (1) Industrial turbines
   (2) Internal combustion engines
4. Electrical Equipment
   (1) Equipment for transmission and distribution of electricity
   (2) Electrical motors
   (3) Electrical furnaces
   (4) X-ray equipment
   (5) Electronic components and equipment
5. Transportation
   (1) Mechanised sailing vessels upto 1000 DWT
   (2) Ship ancillaries
   (3) Commercial vehicles

6. Industrial Machinery
7. Machine Tools
7A. Jigs, Fixtures, Tools and Dies of Specialised Types
8. Agricultural Machinery
    Tractors and power tillers
9. Earthmoving Machinery
10. Industrial Instruments: indicating, recording and regulating devices for pressure, temperature, rate of flow, weights, levels and the like.
11. Scientific Instruments
12. Nitrogenous and Phosphatic Fertilisers falling under
    (1) Inorganic fertilisers under '18 Fertilisers' in the First Schedule to the IDR Act 1951.
13. Chemicals (other than Fertilisers)
    (1) Inorganic heavy chemicals
    (2) Organic heavy chemicals
    (3) Fine chemicals, including photographic chemicals
    (4) Synthetic resins and plastics
    (5) Synthetic rubbers
    (6) Man-made fibres
    (7) Industrial explosives
    (8) Insecticides, fungicides, weedicides and the like
    (9) Synthetic detergents
    (10) Miscellaneous chemicals (for industrial use only)
14. Drugs and Pharmaceuticals
    (a) Drug intermediates from the basic stage for production of high technology bulk drugs; and
    (b) High technology bulk drugs from basic stage and formulation based thereon with an overall ratio of bulk consumption (from own manufacture) to formulation from all sources of 1:5.
15. Paper and Pulp Including Paper Products
16. Automobile Tyres and Tubes
17. Plate Glass
18. Ceramics
    (1) Refractories
    (2) Furnace lining bricks-acidic, basic and neutral
19. Cement Products
    (1) Portland cement
    (2) Asbestos cement

Source: Government of India, Guidelines for Industries, (1979), *op.cit.*, Section II, pp 8-9.

Appendix I – **Industries, 1982** (Revised list)

I. **Metallurgical** Industries
   1. **Ferro Alloys**
   2. Automotive casting, SG iron castings, Steel castings and Steel forgings
   3. Non-ferrous metals and their alloys including aluminium foils
   4. Sponge iron and Pelletisation

II. Boilers and Steam Generating Plants

III. Prime Movers other than Electrical Generators
   1. Industrial turbines
   2. Internal combustion engines
   3. Alternate energy systems like solar, wind, etc. and equipment therefor
   4. Gas/hydro/steam turbines from 20 MW to 60 MW

IV. Electrical Equipment
   1. Equipment for transmission and distribution of electricity including power and distribution of transformers, power relays, HT switch gears, synchronous condensors
   2. Electrical motors
   3. Electrical furnaces including industrial furnaces
   4. X-ray equipment
   5. Electronic components and equipment
   6. Component wires for manufacture of lead-in-wires
   7. Hydro/steam/gas generators from 20 MW to 60 MW

V. Transportation
   1. Mechanised sailing vessels upto 10,000 DWT including fishing trawlers
   2. Ship ancillaries
   3. (i) Commercial vehicles, public transport vehicles including automotive commercial three-wheeler jeep type vehicles, industrial locomotives
      (ii) Personal transport vehicles
         (a) passenger cars
         (b) automotive two-wheelers and three-wheelers. Regarding two-wheelers only expansion of existing units subject to an export obligation of 25% on additional capacity.
      (iii) Specialised automotive components such as pistons and piston rings, fuel injection equipment, auto-electricals, such as starter motors, generators, spark plugs, rear axle assembly, brake and

clutch assembly, tyre/tube valves, wheels for automobiles and bimetal bearings.

VI. Industrial Machinery including Specialised Equipment
 1. High performance and high fidelity industrial valves as may be specified by the Ministry of Industry
 2. Centralised lubrication systems
 3. Gears, gear boxes and couplings
 4. Rolls for paper mills, rolls for rolling mills
 5. Pollution control equipment
 6. Proces equipment for utilization of recycling of wastes

VII. Machine Tools including Controls and Acessories
 1. Jigs, fixtures, tools and dies of specialised types and cross land tooling
 2. Engineering production aids such as cutting and forming tools, patterns and dies and mining tools

VIII. Agricultural Machinery
 1. Tractors

IX. Earth Moving Machinery
 1. Earth moving machinery and construction machinery and components thereof

X. Industrial Instruments
 1. Indicating, recording and regulating devices for pressure, temperature, rate of flow, weights, levels and the like

XI. Scientific and Electromedical Instruments and Laboratory Equipment

XII. Nitrogenous & Phosphatic Fertilizers (falling under)
 1. Inorganic fertilizers under '18 Fertilizers' in the First Schedule to the IDR Act, 1951.

XIII. Chemicals (Other than fertilizers)
 1. Heavy organic chemicals including petro-chemicals
 2. Heavy inorganic chemicals
 3. Organic fine chemicals
 4. Synthetic resins and plastics
 5. Man-made fibres
 6. Synthetic rubber
 7. Industrial explosives
 8. Technical grade insecticides, **fungicides**, weedicides and the like
 9. Synthetic detergents
 10. Miscellaneous chemicals (for industrial use only) including

i) Catalysts and catalyst supports
ii) Photographic chemicals
iii) Rubber chemicals
iv) Polyols
v) Isocyanates, Urethanes, etc.
vi) Speciality chemicals for enhanced oil recovery
vii) Heating fluids
viiii) Coal for distillation and products therefrom
xiv) Alkali/acid resisting cement compound
xv) Leather chemicals and auxiliaries

XIV. Drugs and Pharmaceuticals
For FERA Drug Companies
(a) Drug intermediates from the basic stage for production of high technology bulk drugs
(b) High technology bulk drugs from basic stages and formulations based thereon with an overall ratio of bulk drug consumption (from own manufacture) to formulations from all sources of 1:5

For Non-FERA MRTP Companies
All bulk drugs and formulations with an overall ratio of 1:10 between the value of production of bulk drugs and of formulations

XV. Paper
1. Paper and Pulp including paper products
2. Industrial laminates

XVI. Rubber Products
1. Automobile tyres and tubes, including automobile tyre tube valves
2. Rubberised heavy duty industrial beltings of all types
3. Rubberised conveyor beltings
4. Rubber reinforced and lined fire fighting hose pipes

XVII. Plate glass
1. Float glass
2. Toughened glass insulators
3. Glass fibres of all types

XVIII. Ceramics
1. Refractories
2. **Furnace lining bricks – acidic, basic and neutral**
3. **Ceramic fibres**

XIX. Cement Products
1. **Portland cement**
2. **Gypsum boards, wall boards and the like**

XX. High Technology Reproduction and Multiplication Equipment
XXI. Carbon and Carbon Products
1. Graphite electrodes and anodes
2. Impervious graphite blocks and sheets
XXII. Pretensioned High Pressure RCC Pipes
XXIII. Printing Machinery
1. Web-Fed high speed offset rotary printing machines having output of 30,000 or more impressions per hour
2. Photo composing/type setting machines
3. Multi-colour sheet-fed offset printing machines of sizes 18" x 25" and above
4. High speed Rotogravure printing machines having output of 30,000 or more impressions per hour
XXIV. Rubber Machinery

Source: Indian Investment Centre.

Appendix II: Illustrative List of Industries Where No Foreign Collaboration, Financial Or Technical, Is Considered Necessary (1978)

1. Metallurgical Industries
   Ferrous: Ordinary Castings, Bright Bars, Structurals, Welded CI Steel Pipes and Tubes

   Non-ferrous: Antimony, Sodium Metal, Electrical Resistance Heating (nickel free alloy), Aluminium litho plates

2. Electrical Equipment
   Electrical fans, Common domestic appliances, Common types of winding wires and strips, Iron clad switches, AC motors, Cables and Distribution transformers

3. Electronic Components and Equipments
   General purpose transistors & Diodes, Paper, Mica and Variable Capacitors, T.V. Receivers, Tape Recorders, Teleprinters, P.A. Systems, Record Players/Changers

4. Scientific and Industrial Instruments
   Non-specialised types of valves, meters, weighing machinery, and mathematical, surveying and drawing instruments

5. Transportation
   Railway wagons, Bicycles

6. Building and constructional machinery, Oil mill machinery, Conventional rice mill machinery, Sugar

machinery, Tea processing machinery, General purpose machinery

7. Machine Tools
Forged hand tools, General purpose machine tools

8. Agricultural Machinery
Tractor drawn implements, Power tillers, Foodgrain dryers, Agricultural implements

9. Miscellaneous Mechanical Engineering Industries

10. Commercial, Office and Household Equipments of Common Use

11. Medical and Surgical Appliances

12. Fertilizers
Single super phosphate, Granulated fertilizers

13. Chemicals (Other than Fertilizers)
Acetic acid; Acetanilide; Ethyl Chloride; Viscose Filament Yarn/Staple fibre; Melatin technical; Sulphate of alumina; Potassium Chlorate; Fatty acids & Glycerine; Butyl Titanate; Warfarin; Silica gel; Lindane: Endosulfan; Phanthoate; Nitrofen, Ethyl ether; Plastipeel.

14. Dye-stuffs
Benzidine; O-Toludine; Carbozole Dioxazine violet pigment; Cadmium sulphide orange

15. Drugs and Pharmaceuticals
Caffeine (natural); Phenyl Butazone; Tolbutamide; Paracetamol; Phanacetin; Senna extract; Diasogenin; Clofibrate; 4-Hydroxy Cumarin; Xenthopotoxin; Calcium Gluconate; Choline Chloride; Glyceryl Gualacolate; Phenylethyl biguanide hydrochloride; Scopolamine hydro-bromide; Niacinamide; Ortholelyl biguanide; Colchicine; Diazepam; Sorbitol from dextrose monohydrate; Berberine hydrochloride; Belladonna; Acriflavine; Calcium hypophosphite; Chlordiazepoxide

16. Paper and Pulp including Paper Products

17. Consumer Goods

18. Vegetable Oils and Vanaspati

19. Rubber Industries
Viscose tyre yarn; Metal bonded rubber; Latex foam; Roberised fabrics; Bicycle tyres and tubes

20. Leather, Leather Goods and Pickers
Belting-leather; Cotton and hair finished leather; Pickers; Picking bands; Vegetable tanning extracts; Fat liquors other than synthetic

21. Glass and Ceramics

22. Cement and Gypsum Products

Note: List is illustrative and not exhaustive. Clarification of details within the broad headings is the responsibility of Administrative Ministries.

Source: Government of India, *Guidelines for Industries* (1979), *op.cit.*, Part I, Section I, pp 28-29.

Appendix III: Section 29 of the Foreign Exchange Regulation Act (1973)

(29) (1) Without prejudice to the provisions of section 28 and section 47 and notwithstanding anything contained in any other provision of this Act or the provisions of the Companies Act, 1956, a person resident outside India (whether a citizen of India or not) or a person, who is not a citizen of India but is not incorporated under any law in force in India or in which the non-resident interest is more than forty per cent, or any branch of such company, shall not, except with the general or special permission of the Reserve Bank, -

- (a) carry on in India, or establish in India a branch, office or other place of business for carrying on any activity of a trading, commercial or industrial nature, other than an activity for the carrying on of which permission of the Reserve Bank has been obtained under section 28; or

- (b) acquire the whole or any part of any undertaking in India of any person or company carrying on any trade, commerce or industry or purchase the shares in India of any such company.

(2) (a) Where any person or company (including its branch) referred to in subsection (1) carries on any activity referred to in clause (a) of that subsection at the commencement of this Act or has established a branch, office or other place of business for the carrying on of such activity at such commencement, then, such person or company (including its branch) may make an application to the Reserve Bank within a period of six months from such commencement or such further period as the Reserve Bank may allow in this behalf for permission to continue to carry on such activity or to continue the establishment of the branch, office or other place of business for the carrying on of such activity as the case may be.

- (b) Every application made under clause (a) shall be in such form and contain such particulars as may be specified by the Reserve Bank.

- (c) Where any application has been made under clause

(a), the Reserve Bank may, after making such inquiry as it may deem fit, either allow the application subject to such conditions, if any, as the Reserve Bank may think fit to impose or reject the application:

Provided that no application shall be rejected under this clause unless the parties who may be affected by such rejection have been given a reasonable opportunity for making a representation in the matter.

(d) Where an application is rejected by the Reserve Bank under clause (c), the person or company (including its branch) concerned shall discontinue such activity or close down the branch, office or other place of business established for the carrying on of such activity, as the case may be, on the expiry of a period of ninety days or such other later date as may be specified by the Reserve Bank from the date of receipt by such person or company (including its branch) of the communication conveying such rejection.

(e) Where no application has been made under clause (a) by any person or company (including its branch), the Reserve Bank may, by order, direct such person or company (including its branch) to discontinue such activity or to close down the branch, office or other place of business established for the carrying on of such activity, as the case may be, on the expiry of such period as may be specified in the direction:

Provided that no direction shall be made under this clause unless the parties who may be affected by such direction have been given a reasonable opportunity for making a representation in the matter.

(3) Notwithstanding anything contained in sub-section (2), the Reserve Bank may, having regard to –

(i) the fact that any person or company (including its branch), referred to in sub-section (1), is carrying on any activity referred to in clause (a) of that sub-section at the commencement of this Act or has established a branch, office or other place of business for the carrying on of such activity at such commencement, in either case, in pursuance of any permission or licence granted by the Central Government; and

(ii) the nature of the activity which is being, or intended to be, carried on by such person or company (including its branch), by order, exempt –

(a) such person or company (including its branch); or

(b) any class of such persons or companies (including their branches),

in relation to such activity as may be specified in the order, from the operation of the provisions of sub-section (2) subject to such conditions as may be specified in the order:

Provided that the Reserve Bank shall not make any order under this sub-section in a case where the activity which is being, or intended to be, carried on is solely of a trading nature.

(4) (a) Where at the commencement of this Act any person or company (including its branch) referred to in sub-section (1) holds any shares in India of any company referred to in clause (b) of that sub-section, then, such person or company (including its branch) shall not be entitled to continue to hold such shares unless before the expiry of a period of six months from such commencement or such further period as the Reserve Bank may allow in this behalf such person or company (including its branch) has made an application to the Reserve Bank in such form and containing such particulars as may be specified by the Reserve Bank for permission to continue to hold such shares.

(b) Where an application has been made under clause (a), the Reserve Bank may, after making such inquiry as it may deem fit, either allow the application subject to such conditions, if any, as the Reserve Bank may think fit to impose or reject the application:

Provided that no application shall be rejected under this clause unless the parties who may be affected by such rejection have been given a reasonable opportunity for making a representation in the matter.

(c) Where an application has been rejected under clause (b), or where no application has been made under clause (a), the Reserve Bank may, if it is of opinion that it is expedient so to do for the purpose of conserving the foreign exchange, direct such person or company (including its branch) to sell or procure the sale of such shares:

Provided that no direction shall be made under this clause unless notice of such direction for a period of not less than ninety days has been given to the person or company (including its branch) to be affected by such direction.

Appendix IV: Data Sources

The data used as basis for this book have been collected from several sources. Most important are comprehensive discussions with business representatives and government officials. During visits to India in 1977, 1979, 1983 and 1988, a total of more than 100 leading executives and decision-makers were interviewed. They represented TNC branches and subsidiaries; Indian controlled companies with foreign collaboration; all major chambers of commerce and industry; and all organs of government involved in regulation of foreign companies and transfer of capital and technology.

Other sources include commission reports; legal documents; statistics compiled by various departments and agencies; company annual reports and balance sheets; press reports; and studies published in periodicals and books. A list of published documents referred to is attached at the end of this report.

The Corporate Information System at the Indian Institute of Public Administration, New Delhi, proved extremely useful. The System includes a comprehensive collection of company annual reports, a balance sheet library, a press clippings section and computer files containing detailed and systematic information about the corporate sector in India. I was given access to all these data on the sole condition that I would not compile and publish any tables on the basis of the computer files prior to the publication of the data concerned by the Corporate Studies Group.

Amongst the other institutions and agencies which greatly facilitated data collection should be mentioned the Indian Investment Centre, New Delhi; the Reserve Bank of India, Bombay; the Associated Chambers of Commerce and Industry, New Delhi; the Organisation of Pharmaceutical Producers of India, Bombay; the MRTP Library, New Delhi; and the Bombay Stock Exchange Library. While collecting information on individual TNCs, their performance and corporate strategies in relation to India, I also benefitted from using the New York Times' Information Bank, access to which was provided free of charge by the State Library, Aarhus.

As a condition for granting the interviews mentioned above, most business executives requested that neither their names nor those of their companies would appear in any published report. Similarly, most government officials preferred to remain anonymous. In agreement with these conditions, information obtained during interviews are reproduced in this book in such a manner that individual companies and persons cannot be identified. This is in keeping with the whole approach adopted here, the aim of which is to identify deficiencies in the regulatory arrangements, not the specific circumventions of individual companies. However, where such circumventions are both typical and known from published sources, individual companies have been mentioned by name.

Appendix V. Table A. The Structure of Expenditure in Foreign Currency. Chemicals. 1975-76 to 1980-81.

	1975-76 Rs.lakhs	% of total	1976-77 Rs.lakhs	% of total	1977-78 Rs.lakhs	% of total	1978-79 Rs.lakhs	% of total	1979-80 Rs.lakhs	% of total	1980-81 Rs.lakhs	% of total
Total expenditure	127,66	100.0	149,20	100.0	211,47	100.0	222,50	100.0	280,15	100.0	329,61	100.0
Imports	108,39	84.9	110,19	73.9	180,87	85.5	179,67	80.8	246,10	87.8	297,89	90.4
- of which												
Raw materials	93,83	73.5	94,81	63.5	149,35	70.6	145,88	65.6	207,11	73.9	235,47	71.4
Capital goods	7,96	6.2	6,20	4.2	16,38	7.7	15,74	7.1	13,80	4.9	39,21	11.9
Stores and spares and others	6,60	5.2	9,18	6.2	15,14	7.2	18,05	8.1	25,19	9.0	23,21	7.0
Remittances	19,29	15.1	39,01	26.1	30,60	14.5	42,82	19.2	34,04	12.2	31,72	9.6
- of which												
Dividends	6,64	5.2	14,88	10.0	18,34	8.7	26,44	11.9	17,69	6.3	13,94	4.2
Royalty	1,85	1.4	1,27	0.9	1,51	0.7	1,06	0.5	84	0.3	76	0.2
Technical fees and other fees	1,98	1.6	14,15	9.5	1,77	0.8	3,42	1.5	3,14	1.1	6,11	1.9
Other remittances	8,82	6.9	8,71	5.8	8,98	4.2	11,90	5.3	12,37	4.4	10,91	3.3

Sources: Calculated on the basis of information provided in RBI, 'Finances of Medium and Large Public Limited Companies', 1977-78: *Reserve Bank of India Bulletin*, May, 1980: 1980-81: *Reserve Bank of India Bulletin*, July, 1983.

Appendix V. Table B. The Structure of Expenditure in Foreign Currency. Engineering. 1975-76 to 1980-81.

	1975-76 Rs.lakhs	% of total	1976-77 Rs.lakhs	% of total	1977-78 Rs.lakhs	% of total	1978-79 Rs.lakhs	% of total	1979-80 Rs.lakhs	% of total	1980-81 Rs.lakhs	% of total
Total expenditure	265,08	100.0	279,66	100.0	288,07	100.0	344,20	100.0	504,53	100.0	614,48	100.0
Imports	235,30	88.8	246,47	88.1	247,39	85.9	293,28	85.2	446,54	88.5	536,96	87.4
- of which												
Raw materials	174,61	65.9	180,32	64.5	176,58	61.3	210,80	61.2	326,97	64.8	367,47	59.8
Capital goods	25,94	9.8	30,00	10.7	31,55	11.0	32,72	9.5	39,88	7.9	54,78	8.9
Stores and spares and others	34,75	13.1	36,15	12.9	39,26	13.6	49,76	14.5	79,69	15.8	114,71	18.7
Remittances	29,78	11.2	33,20	11.9	40,70	14.1	50,91	14.8	57,99	11.5	77,53	12.6
- of which												
Dividends	6,91	2.6	9,66	3.5	12,38	4.3	13,42	3.9	14,92	3.0	17,22	2.8
Royalty	5,01	1.9	6,61	2.4	6,21	2.2	5,43	1.6	7,69	1.5	7,86	1.3
Technical fees and other fees	4,99	1.9	4,06	1.5	3,80	1.3	3,91	1.1	4,91	1.0	6,59	1.1
Other remittances	12,87	4.9	12,87	4.6	18,31	6.4	28,15	8.2	30,47	6.0	45,86	7.5

Sources: As for Table A.

Appendix V. Table C. The Structure of Expenditure in Foreign Currency for Group III – Industries a), 1975-76 to 1980-81.

	1975-76 Rs.lakhs	% of total	1976-77 Rs.lakhs	% of total	1977-78 Rs.lakhs	% of total	1978-79 Rs.lakhs	% of total	1979-80 Rs.lakhs	% of total	1980-81 Rs.lakhs	% of total
Total expenditure	70,41	100.0	92,37	100.0	243,61	100.0	244,28	100.0	209,81	100.0	197,78	100.0
Imports	63,06	89.6	82,33	89.1	232,22	95.3	233,34	95.5	198,28	94.5	184,74	93.4
- of which												
Raw materials	47,03	66.8	63,88	69.2	210,27	86.3	203,63	83.4	159,59	76.1	133,52	67.5
Capital goods	9,15	13.0	11,01	11.9	13,63	5.6	18,18	7.4	23,80	11.3	33,66	17.0
Stores and spares and others	6,88	9.8	7,44	8.1	8,32	3.4	11,53	4.7	14,89	7.1	17,56	8.9
Remittances	7,31	10.4	10,06	10.9	11,40	4.7	10,92	4.5	11,51	5.5	13,06	6.6
- of which												
Dividends	1,37	1.9	3,76	4.1	4,19	1.7	4,41	1.8	3,08	1.5	3,33	1.7
Royalty	50	0.7	56	0.6	40	0.2	37	0.2	12	0.1	38	0.2
Technical fees and other fees	7	0.1	20	0.2	4	0.0	13	0.1	36	0.2	9	0.0
Other remittances	5,37	7.6	5,54	6.0	6,77	2.8	6,01	2.5	7,95	3.8	9,26	4.7

Sources: As for Table A.
a) Group III – industries comprise foodstuffs, textiles, tobacco, leather and products thereof.

Selected Bibliography

Agrawal, H.P., *Business Collaboration in India*, New Delhi, Aruna, 1979.

Bagchi, A.K., *Transnational Corporations as Transferors of Capital and Technology in India: Some Critical Issues*, Calcutta, Centre for Studies in Social Sciences, n.d. (1982).

Bagchi, A.K. et al., 'Indian Patents Act and Its Relation to Technological Development in India', *EPW*, February 18, 1984.

Bagchi, A.K., 'Foreign Collaboration in Indian Industry', *EPW*, May 24, 1986.

Behara, Meenakshi, 'Welcome Back Yanks?', *Business India*, Sept 10-23, 1984.

Bhaskar, R.N., 'Wimco's March Beyond the Match', *Business India*, Aug. 12-25, 1985.

Bhushan, B., 'The New Deals', *Business India*, May 9-22, 1983.

Brooke, Michael Z. & H. Lee Remmers, *The Strategy of Multional Enterprice, Organization and Finance*, London, Pitman, 1978.

Chaudhuri, Sudip, 'Financing of Growth of Transnational Corporations in India, 1956-75', *EPW*, Aug 18, 1979.

Chitale, V.P., *Foreign Technology in India*, New Delhi, Economic and Scientific Research Foundation, 1973.

Corporate Studies Group, *Functioning of the Industrial Licensing System. A Report*, New Delhi, Indian Institute of Public Administration, 1983.

Dhar, Biswajit, *Foreign Controlled Companies in India: An Attempt at Identification*, New Delhi, Indian Institute of Public Administration, 1987.

Dunning, J.H., 'Explaining Changing Patterns of International Production: In Defence of the Eclectic Theory', *Oxford Bulletin of Economics and Statistics*, Vol. 41, No. 4 (1979).

Selected Bibliography

Economic Times Research Bureau, *Finances of Major Pharmaceutical Companies in India*, Bombay, n.d. (1982).

Eldridge, P.J., *The Politics of Foreign Aid in India*, London, Weidenfeld and Nicolson, 1969.

Encarnation, Dennis & Suchil Vachani, 'Foreign Ownership: When Hosts Change the Rules', *Harward Business Review*, 1985, No. 5.

Fröbel, Folker; Jürgen Heinrich and Otto Kreye, *Die neue internationale Arbeitsteilung. Strukturelle Arbeitslosigkeit in den Industrieländern und die Industrialisierung der Entwicklungsländern*, Hamburg, Rowohlt, 1977.

Government of India, *Industrial Policy Resolution of 1948*, in: Constituent Assembly of India (Legislative), Debates, Vol. V, No. 1, (6th April 1948).

Government of India, *The Industries (Development and Regulations) Act, 1951* (As Modified up to 1st Dec. 1965), Delhi, 1966.

Government of India, Ministry of Finance, *India. Pocket Book of Economic Information*, 1968.

Government of India, *Foreign Exchange Regulation Act, 1973*.

Government of India, *Economic Survey 1982-83*, Delhi, 1983.

Government of India, Ministry of Law, Justice and Company Affairs, *The Monopolies and Restrictive Trade Practices Act, 1969 (As modified up to the 1st October, 1976)*. Delhi, 1976.

Government of India, Ministry of Law, Justice and Company Affairs, *The Monopolies and Restrictive Trade Practices Act. Rules and Regulations*, New Delhi, 1977.

Government of India, Ministry of Industry, Directorate General of Technical Development, *Handbook of Foreign Collaboration 1980*, New Delhi 1980.

Government of India, Ministry of Industry, *Guidelines for Industries 1976-77, Guidelines for Industries (1979), Guidelines for Industries 1982-83*, New Delhi, 1976, 1979, 1982.

Government of India, Ministry of Petroleum and Chemicals, *Report of the Committee on Drugs and Pharmaceutical Industry*, Delhi, April, 1975.

Government of West Bengal, *The IMF Loan. Facts and Issues*, Calcutta, 1981.

Goyal, S.K., *The Impact of Foreign Subsidiaries on India's Balance of Payments*, Indian Institute of Public Administration, New Delhi, 1979.

Goyal, S.K., *Monopoly Capital and Public Policy*, New Delhi, Allied Publishers, 1979.

Goyal, S.K., *Multinational Corporations in India: The Need for a Realistic Policy Framework*, New Delhi, Indian Institute of Public Administration, n.d. (1980).

Goyal, S.K., *A Preliminary Survey of Excess Industrial Capacities with the Indian Corporate Sector*, New Delhi, Indian Institute of Public Administration, 1980.

Goyal, S.K., *Some Aspects of the Operations of Multinational Corporations in India*, New Delhi, Indian Institute of Public Administration, n.d. (1981).

Goyal, S.K., *The New International Economic Order and Transnational Corporations*, New Delhi, 1982 (Mimeo).

Grieco, Joseph M., 'Between Dependence and Autonomy: India's Experience with the International Computer Industry', *International Organization*, Vol. 36, No. 3 (1982).

Hoffman, L. et al., *Technology Transfer and Investment. European Community - India*, (Joint Report on the EC/India Project on the Problems and Perspectives of the Transfer of Technology between Firms in the European Community and India), Berlin, 1984.

India International Inc., *Doing Business Collaborations in India* (Prepared for U.S. Department of State and the Overseas Private Investment Corporation), Washington, D.C., 1985.

Indian Investment Centre, *Taxes and Incentives. A guide for investors 1979-80*, New Delhi, 1979.

Indian Investment Centre, *Investing in India: A Guide to Entrepreneurs*, New Delhi, 1987.

Indian Investment Centre, *Directory of Foreign Collaboration in India: India-Japan*, Vol. IV A (1981-1984), New Delhi, 1987.

Indo-American Chamber of Commerce, *Indo-U.S. Joint Ventures: Partners in Progress*, Bombay, 1982.

Joint CTC/ESCAP Unit on Transnational Corporations, *Monitoring and Regulating Transnational Corporations in India*, Bangkok, 1980.

Kapur, S.L., *Policy, Procedures and Problems Regarding Import of Technology by India*, Vienna, UNIDO, 1982.

Khanna, Sushil, *Transnational Corporations and Technology Transfer: Contours of Dependence in the Indian Petrochemical Industry*, Calcutta, Indian Institute of Management, n.d. (1982).

Kidron, Michael, *Foreign Investments in India*, London, Oxford University Press, 1965.

Kirchbach, Friedrich von, *Economic Policies Towards Transnational Corporations. The Experience of the ASEAN Countries*, Baden-Baden, Nomos, 1983.

Kochanek, Stanley A., *Business and Politics in India*, Berkeley, University of California Press, 1974.

Kumar, Nagesh & K.M. Chenoy, 'Multinationals and Self-reliance: A case Study of the Drugs and Pharmaceutical Industry', *Social Scientist*, No. 107 (1982).

Kumar, Nagesh, 'Regulating Multinational Monopolies in India', *EPW*, May 29, 1982.
Kumar, Nagesh, 'Technology Policy in India: An Overview of its Evolution and an Assessment', in: P.R. Brahmananda and V.R.Panchamukhi (eds.), *The Development Process of the Indian Economy*, Bombay, Himalaya, 1987.
Kumar, Nagesh, *Multinational Enterprises and Export Promotion. The Case of India*, New Delhi, Research and Information System for Non-Aligned and Other Developing Countries, 1987.

Lall, Sanjaya, 'Monopolistic Advantages and Foreign Involvement by US Manufacturing Industry', *Oxford Economic Papers*, Vol. 32, No. 1, (1980).
Lall, Sanjaya, 'International Technology Market and Developing Countries', *EPW*, Annual Number, Febr. 1980.
Lall, Sanjaya, & Sharif Mohammad, 'Multinationals in Indian Big Business', *Journal of Development Economics*, Vol. 13 (1983).
Lall, Sanjaya & Paul Streeten, *Foreign Investment, Transnationals and Developing Countries*, London, Macmillan, 1977.

Mani, Sunil, 'Concentration and Marketpower in Indian Automotive Tyre Industry', *EPW*, May 25, 1985.
Martinussen, John, *The Indian State and the Multinational Corporation: Contributions to an Analysis of the Extra - Societal Determination of State Functions*, Aarhus, Institute of Political Science, 1976.
Martinussen, John, *Staten i perifere og post-koloniale samfund Indien og Pakistan* (The State in Peripheral and Post-colonial Societies: India and Pakistan), Aarhus, Politica, 1980.
Martinussen, John, *The Public Industrial Sector in India*, Aarhus, Institute of Political Science, 1980.
Murray, Robin (ed.), *Multinationals Beyond the Market. Intra-firm Trade and Control of Transfer Pricing*, Brighton, Harwester Press, 1981.
Mukherjee, Neela, 'Technical Payments Abroad', *Economic Times*, November 16, 1983.

Narayan, Rajan, 'The Changing Face of Hindustan Lever', *Business India*, July 21-Aug. 3, 1980.

OECD, *International Investment and Multinational Enterprises. Recent International Direct Investment Trends*, Paris, 1981.
Oman, Charles, *New Forms of International Investment in Developing Countries*, Paris, OECD, 1984.
OPPI, *The Pharmaceutical Industry in India. Allegations and Facts*, Bombay, n.d.

Paranjape, H.K., 'India: Control of Restrictive Business Practices', *Journal of World Trade Law*, Vol. 13, No. 3, (May-June 1979).

Paranjape, H.K., 'New Statement of Industrial Policy', *EPW*, Sept. 20, 1980.

Paranjape, H.K., 'The Vanishing MRTP Act: Will only the Grin Remain?', *EPW*, June 5, 1982.

'Pharmaceutical Industry: Mid-term Plan Review', *Commerce*, Febr. 26, 1983.

Rana, Pradumna B., 'Foreign Direct Investment and Economic Growth in the Asian and Pacific Region', *Asian Development Review*, Vol. 5, No. 1 (1987).

Rao, Chalapati, *India's Export Policies and Performance: An Evaluation*, New Delhi, Indian Institute of Public Administration, 1987.

Rath, Ajay Kumar, 'Local and Global Operations of Multinational Corporations: Unilever in India', *Social Scientist*, Vol. 10, No. 10 (1982).

Ravindranath, Sushila, 'Pond's Aroma of Success', *Business India*, July 29-Aug. 11, 1985.

Reserve Bank of India, *India's Foreign Liabilities and Assets 1961-Survey Report*, Bombay, 1964.

Reserve Bank of India, *Foreign Collaboration in Indian Industry. Survey Report*, Bombay, 1968.

Reserve Bank of India, 'Survey of Foreign Financial and Technical Collaboration in Indian Industry 1964-70', *RBI Bulletin*, June 1974.

Reserve Bank of India, 'Finances of Branches of Foreign Controlled Rupee Companies, 1972-73', *RBI Bulletin*, July 1975.

Reserve Bank of India, *Foreign Collaboration in Indian Industry. Second Survey Report 1974*, Bombay n.d. (1975).

Reserve Bank of India, 'India's International Investment Position, 1973-74' *RBI Bulletin*, March 1978.

Reserve Bank of India, 'Foreign Exchange Earnings and Outgo by Medium and Large Processing and Manufacturing Companies, 1975-76 to 1977-78', *RBI Bulletin*, July 1981.

Reserve Bank of India, 'Finances of Medium and Large Public Limited Companies', 1977-78: *RBI Bulletin*, May 1980, 1980-81: *RBI Bulletin*, July 1983.

Reserve Bank of India, 'Trends in Consents for Issue of Capital and Public Response to Capital Issues During 1976-1980', *RBI Bulletin*, Feb. 1982.

Reserve Bank of India, 'Finances of Foreign Controlled Rupee Companies, 1975-76 to 1980-81', *RBI Bulletin*, August 1984.

Reserve Bank of India, 'India's International Investment Position 1977-78 to 1979-80', *RBI Bulletin*, April 1985.

Selected Bibliography

Reserve Bank of India, *Foreign Collaboration in Indian Industry. Fourth Survey Report*, 1985, Bombay 1985.

Robock,H. & Kenneth Simmonds, *International Business and Multinational Enterprises*, Homewood, Ill., Richard D. Irving, 1983 (3rd ed.).

Roy, Subrata, 'The Lever-Lipton Brew', *Business India*, July 4-17, 1983.

Roy, Subrata, 'The Stock Markets: Up, Up and Away', *Business India*, July 29-Aug. 11, 1985.

Roy, Subrata, 'Hindustan Lever: India's Largest Foreign Company', *Business India*, Sept. 23-Oct. 6, 1985.

Subramanian,K.K. & P.Mohanan Pillai, *Multinationals and Indian Export*, New Delhi, Allied Publishers 1979.

Sauvant, Karl P. and Farid G.Lavipour (eds), *Controlling Multinational Enterprises: Problems, Strategies, Counterstrategies*, Boulder, Colorado, Westview Press, 1976.

Tanzer, Michael, *The Political Economy of International Oil and the Underdeveloped Countries*, Boston, Beacon Press, 1970.

Tsurumi, Yoshi, *Multinational Management. Business Strategy and Government Policy*, Cambridge, Mass., Ballinger, 1984.

Tyebjee, Tyzoon T., 'Catalysing Enterpreneurship and Innovation', *Business India*, Jan. 14-27, 1985.

UNCTC, *National Legislation and Regulations Relating to Transnational Corporations*, New York, 1978.

UNCTC, *Transnational Corporations in World Development. Third Survey*, New York, 1983.

UNCTC, *National Legislation and Regulations Relating to Transnational Corporations* (Second Survey),New York, 1983.

UNCTC, *Transnational Corporations and Technology Transfer: Effects and Policy Issues*, New York, 1987.

UNCTC, *Trends and Issues in Foreign Direct Investment and Related Flows*, New York, 1985.

UN, Dept. of Economic and Social Affairs, *Multinational Corporations in World Development*, New York, 1973.

UN, ECOSOC, *Transnational Corporations in World Development: A Re-examination*, New York, 1978.

UNCTAD, *Control in India of Restrictive Business Practices*, (prepared by H.K.Paranjape), Geneve, 1978.

UNCTAD, *The Implementation of Transfer of Technology Regulations: A Preliminary Analysis of the Experience of Latin America, India and Philippines*, Geneva, 1980.

Vedavalli,R., *Private Foreign Investment and Economic Development. A Case Study of Petroleum in India*, Cambridge University Press, 1977.

Vernon, Raymond, *Sovereignty at Bay. The Multinational Spread of US Enterprises*, Harmondsworth, Penguin, 1973.

Vernon, Raymond, 'The Product Cycle Hypothesis in a New International Environment', *Oxford Bulletin of Economics and Statistics*, Vol. 41, No. 4 (1979).

Wallace, Cynthia Day, *Legal Control of the Multinational Enterprise*, The Hague, Martinus Nijhoff, 1983.

World Bank, *World Development Report 1985*, London, Oxford University Press, 1985.

Periodicals

Assocham Parliamentary Digest, New Delhi.
Business India, Bombay.
Commerce, Bombay.
Economic and Political Weekly, Bombay.
Economic Times, Bombay and New Delhi.
Far Eastern Economic Review, Hong Kong.
Financial Times, London.
Finance and Development, Washington, D.C.
Government of India, Office of the Controller of Capital Issues. *Quarterly Statistics on the Working of Capital Issues Control*, New Delhi.
Monthly Newsletter, Indian Investment Centre, New Delhi.
Reserve Bank of India Bulletin, Bombay.
Reserve Bank of India Annual Reports, Bombay.
Social Scientist, New Delhi.
Statesman, Calcutta.